Sunday Missal for Young Catholics 2013

I want to know Jesus better.

This missal will help you take part in the Mass on Sundays and important feast days. Pages 2 to 32 contain the words and explain the gestures that are the same for every Mass. The rest of the book gives you the readings and prayers for each Sunday of the year.

Look over the readings with your family before you go to church. This is an excellent way to use this book and a wonderful way to prepare for Mass.

The most important thing about this little book is that it will help you to *know Jesus better*. Jesus came to bring God's love into the world. And his Spirit continues to fill us with love for one another.

We hope the short notes in this book will help you to participate more fully in the Mass. May the Mass become an important part of your life as you grow up, and may the readings and prayers you find in this missal inspire you to love and serve others just as Jesus did.

What we need to celebrate the Mass

A **priest** who makes Jesus present and acts in his name.

The **altar** is the table where the priest consecrates bread and wine.

A group of Christians. You are a Christian by your baptism.

Books with prayers (the missal) and readings (the lectionary).

Two **cruets**, or small containers, one full of water and the other full of wine.

Holy vessels

chalice

ciborium

paten

Bread and wine

The Mass is the commemoration of what Jesus did during the Last Supper with his disciples, before he died. The bread is shaped like a small disk and is called a "host."

The **ambo** is the place where the Word of God is proclaimed.

The four main parts of the Mass

On the following pages you will find the words that the priest says and the responses we say together during each part of the Mass. You will also find explanations and responses to many questions that people ask about the Mass.

Gathering Prayers

The Lord brings us together.
We ask God for forgiveness.
We give glory to God.

The Word

We listen to the Word of God.
We profess our faith.
We pray for the whole world.

The Eucharist

We offer bread and wine to God.
We give thanks to God.
We say the Lord's Prayer.
We share the peace of Christ.
We receive Jesus in communion.

Sending Forth

The Lord sends us home to live the Gospel.

The Lord brings us together

We come together in church with family, friends, neighbours, and strangers. We are here because Jesus has invited us to be here.

When the priest comes in, we stand and sing. Then we make the sign of the cross along with the priest.

Priest: In the name of the Father, and of the Son, and of the Holy Spirit.

Everyone: Amen.

Sometimes, the words can change a bit, but usually the priest will say:

Priest: The grace of our Lord Jesus Christ, and the love of God, and the communion of the Holy Spirit be with you all.

Everyone: And with your spirit.

Why do we celebrate Mass on Sunday?

Jesus rose from the dead on Sunday, the day after the Sabbath. This is why Christians gather on that day. Over time, people started to call it "the Lord's day."

Why do we celebrate Mass in a church?

Churches are built specially for Christians to gather in. If needed, Mass can be celebrated in other places: a home, a school, a plaza, a jail, a hospital, a park...

Why do we need a priest to celebrate Mass?

We believe that Jesus is present in the person of the priest when Christians gather for the Mass. He presides over the celebration of the Lord's supper in the name of Jesus Christ.

Standing

We stand to welcome Jesus who is present among us when we gather in his name.

The sign of the cross

With our right hand we make the sign of the cross (from our forehead to our chest, from our left shoulder to our right) and say "In the name of the Father, and of the Son, and of the Holy Spirit." This is how all Catholic prayer begins.

Singing

This is a joyful way to pray together.

5

Gathering Prayers

We ask God for forgiveness

We speak to God and we recognize that we have done wrong. We ask forgiveness for our misdeeds. God, who knows and loves us, forgives us.

Priest: Brothers and sisters, let us acknowledge our sins, and so prepare ourselves to celebrate the sacred mysteries.

We silently recognize our faults and allow God's loving forgiveness to touch us.

Everyone: I confess to almighty God, and to you, my brothers and sisters, that I have greatly sinned, in my thoughts and in my words, in what I have done and in what I have failed to do, *(tap the heart)* through my fault, through my fault, through my most grievous fault; therefore I ask blessed Mary ever-Virgin, all the Angels and Saints, and you, my brothers and sisters, to pray for me to the Lord our God.

Priest: May almighty God have mercy on us, forgive us our sins, and bring us to everlasting life.

Everyone: Amen.

Priest: Lord, have mercy.

Everyone: Lord, have mercy.

Priest: Christ, have mercy.

Everyone: Christ, have mercy.

Priest: Lord, have mercy.

Everyone: Lord, have mercy.

What does it mean?

Confess

We recognize before others that we have turned away from God, who is love.

Mercy

We know God is full of mercy — that he loves us even when we have sinned. God's mercy is always there for us.

Amen

This is a Hebrew word meaning "Yes, I agree. I commit myself."

Lord

This is a name that we give to God. Christians call Jesus "Lord" because we believe he is the Son of God.

Christ or Messiah

In the Bible, these words designate someone who has been blessed with perfumed oil. This blessing is a sign that God has given a mission to the person. Christians give this name to Jesus.

Gestures

Tapping our heart

This is a way of showing we are very sorry for our sins.

We give glory to God

We recognize God's greatness when we say "Glory to God." This prayer begins with the hymn the angels sang when they announced Jesus' birth to the shepherds.

Everyone: Glory to God in the highest,
and on earth peace to people of good will.

We praise you,
we bless you,
we adore you,
we glorify you,
we give you thanks for your great glory,
Lord God, heavenly King,
O God, almighty Father.

Lord Jesus Christ, Only Begotten Son,
Lord God, Lamb of God, Son of the Father,
you take away the sins of the world,
    have mercy on us;
you take away the sins of the world,
    receive our prayer;
you are seated at the right hand of the Father,
    have mercy on us.

For you alone are the Holy One,
you alone are the Lord,
you alone are the Most High,
Jesus Christ,
with the Holy Spirit,
in the glory of God the Father.
Amen.

Priest: Let us pray.

The priest invites us to pray. He then says a prayer in the name of all of us, and finishes like this:

Through our Lord Jesus Christ, your Son, who lives and reigns with you in the unity of the Holy Spirit, one God, for ever and ever.

Everyone: Amen.

What does it mean?

Glory

With this word, we indicate the greatness of a person. It shows that a person is important. When we say "Glory to God" we are recognizing that God is important in our lives.

Praise

To praise is to speak well and enthusiastically of someone.

Almighty

When we say that God is almighty, we mean that nothing is impossible for God.

Sins of the world

This expression refers to all the evil that is done in the world.

Holy Spirit

This is the Spirit of God, our heavenly guide, who fills us with love for Jesus.

We listen to the Word of God

This is the moment when we listen to several readings from the Bible. We welcome God who speaks to us today.

You can follow the readings in this book. Look for the Sunday that corresponds to today's date.

The first two readings

We sit down for these readings. The first reading is usually taken from the Old Testament. The second is from a letter written by an apostle to the first Christians. Between these two readings, we pray with the responsorial Psalm, which we do best when it is sung.

The Gospel

We stand and sing Alleluia! as we prepare to listen carefully to a reading from one of the Gospels.

Priest: The Lord be with you.

Everyone: And with your spirit.

Priest: A reading from the holy Gospel according to N.

Everyone: Glory to you, Lord.

We trace three small crosses with our thumb: one on our forehead, one on our lips, and another on our heart. When the reading is finished, the priest kisses the book and says:

Priest: The Gospel of the Lord.

Everyone: Praise to you, Lord Jesus Christ.

Homily

We sit down to listen to the comments of the priest, which help us to understand and apply the Word of God in our lives.

What does it mean?

Bible

This is the holy book of all Christians. The Old Testament tells the story of the Covenant God made with the Jewish people before Jesus' time. The New Testament tells the story of the Covenant God made with all people through his son, Jesus Christ.

Psalm

The Psalms are prayers that are found in the Bible. They are meant to be sung.

Alleluia!

This Hebrew word means "May God be praised and thanked."

Gospel

The word "gospel" means "good news." Jesus himself is the Good News who lives with us. The first four books of the New Testament are called "Gospels." They transmit the Good News to us.

Gestures

The sign of the cross which we make on our forehead, lips and heart

means that we want to make the Gospel so much a part of our life that we can proclaim it to all around us with all our heart.

Kissing the book of the Gospels

When the priest does this, he says in a low voice: "Through the words of the Gospel may our sins be wiped away."

11

We profess our faith

We have just listened to the Word of God. To respond to it, with all other Christians in the world, we proclaim the "Creed."

We stand up and profess our faith:

Everyone: I believe in God,
the Father almighty,
Creator of heaven and earth,
and in Jesus Christ, his only Son, our Lord,
who was conceived by the Holy Spirit,
born of the Virgin Mary,
suffered under Pontius Pilate,
was crucified, died and was buried;
he descended into hell;
on the third day he rose again from the dead;
he ascended into heaven,
and is seated at the right hand
    of God the Father almighty;
from there he will come to judge
    the living and the dead.

I believe in the Holy Spirit,
the holy catholic Church,
the communion of saints,
the forgiveness of sins,
the resurrection of the body,
and life everlasting.
Amen.

What does it mean?

Creed

From the Latin verb *credo* that means "I believe." The Creed is the prayer that expresses our faith as Christians.

He suffered

Means the torture Jesus endured before he died on the cross.

Pontius Pilate

This is the name of the Roman governor who ordered that Jesus be crucified.

Crucified

Jesus died by crucifixion. He was nailed to a cross.

Catholic

In Greek, this word means "universal." The Church is open to all people in the world.

Church

The "Church" with a big C refers to the whole Christian community throughout the world. The "church" with a little c is a building where we gather to worship God.

Resurrection

Means coming back to life after having died. God raised Jesus from the dead and gave him new life for ever. Jesus shares that life with us.

We pray for the whole world

This is the moment of the universal Prayer of the Faithful when we present our petitions to God. We pray for the Church, for all of humanity, for those who are sick or lonely, for children who are abandoned, for those who suffer through natural disasters...

After each petition we respond with a phrase, such as:

Everyone: Lord, hear our prayer.

Reader: For the needs of the Church ...

For peace in every country ...

For the hungry and the homeless ...

For ourselves and for all God's children ...

What does it mean?

Some questions

Petitions

Petitions are prayers asking for something specific. Each week at Mass, the petitions change because the needs of the world and our community change. We stand for the petitions and answer "Amen" at the end — to show that our prayers are offered as one.

Why do we call the Prayer of the Faithful "universal"?

It is a universal prayer because it includes everyone: we pray for all the people of the world.

Why do we take up a collection?

Christians help out with the maintenance of the church building and also help people who are in need. Theses gifts are brought to the altar with the bread and the wine.

We offer bread and wine to God

The celebration of the Lord's Supper continues at the altar. Members of the community bring the bread, the wine, and the gifts collected to relieve the needs of the Church and the poor. The priest presents the bread and wine to God and we bless God with him.

We sit down. The priest takes the bread and wine, and lifts them up, saying:

Priest: Blessed are you, Lord God of all creation, for through your goodness we have received the bread we offer you: fruit of the earth and work of human hands, it will become for us the bread of life.

Everyone: Blessed be God for ever.

Priest: Blessed are you, Lord God of all creation, for through your goodness we have received the wine we offer you: fruit of the vine and work of human hands, it will become our spiritual drink.

Everyone: Blessed be God for ever.

The priest washes his hands and says:

Priest: Pray, brothers and sisters, that my sacrifice and yours may be acceptable to God, the almighty Father.

Everyone: May the Lord accept the sacrifice at your hands for the praise and glory of his name, for our good, and the good of all his holy Church.

We stand while the priest, with hands extended, says a prayer over the bread and wine. He usually ends the prayer by saying:

Priest: Through Christ our Lord.

Everyone: Amen.

What does it mean?

Eucharist

A Greek word that means "gratefulness, thanksgiving." The Mass is also called the Eucharist.

Blessed

To bless means to speak well of someone. To bless God is to give thanks for everything God gives us.

Sacrifice

God does not ask for animal sacrifice, as in the old days. Nor does God ask us to die on a cross, like Jesus did. Instead, God asks us to offer our daily life, with Jesus, as a beautiful gift.

Gestures

Procession with the bread and the wine

With this gesture we present to God the fruit of our work and we give thanks for the gift of life that comes from God.

Drops of water in the wine

With this sign, the priest prays that our life be united with God's life.

Washing of hands

Before saying the most important prayer of the Mass, the priest washes his hands and asks God to wash away his sins.

We give thanks to God

At this moment we give thanks to God for his Son, Jesus Christ, for life, and for all that he gives us. This is how the great Eucharistic Prayer begins.

Priest: The Lord be with you.

Everyone: And with your spirit.

Priest: Lift up your hearts.

Everyone: We lift them up to the Lord.

Priest: Let us give thanks to the Lord our God.

Everyone: It is right and just.

Here is one way of celebrating the Eucharist with young Catholics. On page 21, you will find Eucharistic Prayer II which is a common way of celebrating the Eucharist with grown-ups.

Prayer for Mass with Children I

Priest: God our Father, you have brought us here together so that we can give you thanks and praise for all the wonderful things you have done.

We thank you for all that is beautiful in the world and for the happiness you have given us. We praise you for daylight and for your word which lights up our minds. We praise you for the earth, and all the people who live on it, and for our life which comes from you.

We know that you are good. You love us and do great things for us. So we all sing together:

Everyone: Holy, holy, holy Lord, God of power and might, heaven and earth are full of your glory. Hosanna in the highest.

Priest: Father, you are always thinking about your people; you never forget us. You sent us your Son Jesus, who gave his life for us and who came to save us. He cured sick people; he cared for those who were poor and wept with those who were sad. He forgave sinners and taught us to forgive each other. He loved everyone and showed us how to be kind. He took children in his arms and blessed them. So we all sing together:

Everyone: Blessed is he who comes in the name of the Lord. Hosanna in the highest.

Priest: God our Father, all over the world your people praise you. So now we pray with the whole Church: with N., our pope, and N., our bishop. In heaven the blessed Virgin Mary, the apostles and all the saints always sing your praise. Now we join with them and with the angels to adore you as we sing:

Everyone: Holy, holy, holy Lord, God of power and might, heaven and earth are full of your glory.
Hosanna in the highest.
Blessed is he who comes in the name of the Lord.
Hosanna in the highest.

Priest: God our Father, you are most holy and we want to show you that we are grateful.

We bring you bread and wine and ask you to send your Holy Spirit to make these gifts the body and blood of Jesus your Son. Then we can offer to you what you have given to us.

On the night before he died, Jesus was having supper with his apostles. He took bread from the table. He gave you thanks and praise. Then he broke the bread, gave it to his friends, and said:

> Take this, all of you, and eat it:
> this is my body which will be given up for you.

The Eucharist

When supper was ended, Jesus took the cup that was filled with wine. He thanked you, gave it to his friends, and said:

> Take this, all of you, and drink from it:
> this is the cup of my blood,
> the blood of the new and everlasting covenant.
> It will be shed for you and for all
> so that sins may be forgiven.

Then he said to them:

> Do this in memory of me.

We do now what Jesus told us to do. We remember his death and his resurrection and we offer you, Father, the bread that gives us life, and the cup that saves us. Jesus brings us to you; welcome us as you welcome him.

Let us proclaim the mystery of faith:

Everyone: Christ has died, Christ is risen, Christ will come again.

Priest: Father, because you love us, you invite us to come to your table. Fill us with the joy of the Holy Spirit as we receive the body and blood of your Son.

Lord, you never forget any of your children. We ask you to take care of those we love, especially of N. and N.; and we pray for those who have died.

Remember everyone who is suffering from pain or sorrow. Remember Christians everywhere and all other people in the world.

We are filled with wonder and praise when we see what you do for us through Jesus your Son, and so we sing:

Through him, with him, in him, in the unity of the Holy Spirit, all glory and honour is yours, almighty Father, for ever and ever.

Everyone: Amen.
(Turn to page 24)

Prayer II

Priest: It is truly right and just, our duty and our salvation, always and everywhere to give you thanks, Father most holy, through your beloved Son, Jesus Christ, your Word through whom you made all things, whom you sent as our Saviour and Redeemer, incarnate by the Holy Spirit and born of the Virgin.

Fulfilling your will and gaining for you a holy people, he stretched out his hands as he endured his Passion, so as to break the bonds of death and manifest the resurrection.

And so, with the Angels and all the Saints we declare your glory, as with one voice we acclaim:

Everyone: Holy, Holy, Holy Lord God of hosts.
Heaven and earth are full of your glory.
Hosanna in the highest.
Blessed is he who comes in the name of the Lord.
Hosanna in the highest.

Priest: You are indeed Holy, O Lord, the fount of all holiness. Make holy, therefore, these gifts, we pray, by sending down your Spirit upon them like the dewfall, so that they may become for us the Body and Blood of our Lord Jesus Christ.

At the time he was betrayed and entered willingly into his Passion, he took bread and, giving thanks, broke it, and gave it to his disciples, saying:

Take this, all of you, and eat of it,
for this is my Body
which will be given up for you.

In a similar way, when supper was ended, he took the chalice and, once more giving thanks, he gave it to his disciples, saying:

The Eucharist

Priest:
Take this, all of you, and drink from it,
for this is the chalice of my Blood,
the Blood of the new and eternal covenant,
which will be poured out for you and for many
for the forgiveness of sins.
Do this in memory of me.

The mystery of faith.

Everyone: We proclaim your Death, O Lord, and profess your Resurrection until you come again.

Priest: Therefore, as we celebrate the memorial of his Death and Resurrection, we offer you, Lord, the Bread of life and the Chalice of salvation, giving thanks that you have held us worthy to be in your presence and minister to you.

we pray that, partaking of the Body and Blood of Christ, we may be gathered into one by the Holy Spirit.

Lord, your Church, spread throughout the world, and bring her to the fullness of charity, together with N. our Pope and N. our Bishop and all the clergy.

also our brothers and sisters who have fallen asleep in the hope of the resurrection, and all who have died in your mercy: welcome them into the light of your face. Have mercy on us all, we pray, that with the Blessed Virgin Mary, Mother of God, with the blessed Apostles, and all the Saints who have pleased you throughout the ages, we may merit to be coheirs to eternal life, and may praise and glorify you through your Son, Jesus Christ.

him, and with him, and in him, O God, almighty Father, in the unity of the Holy Spirit, all glory and honour is yours, for ever and ever.

Everyone: Amen.

What does it mean?

Covenant

When two people enter into a covenant agreement, they promise to be faithful to one another. God entered into a covenant with us. He is our God and we are his People.

Forgiveness of sins

This is the forgiveness that comes from God, whose love is greater than our sins.

Do this in memory of me

Jesus asked the disciples to remember him by reliving what he said and did during the Last Supper.

The mystery of faith

Together we proclaim our belief in Christ who was born and died for us, rose to life, and will return one day.

Eternal life

This is life with God, which will be given to us fully after death.

Gestures

Extending the hands

When the priest extends his hands, he calls upon the Holy Spirit to consecrate the bread and wine, so that they become for us the Body and Blood of Christ.

Raising the bread

The priest lifts the consecrated bread and then the chalice, so that the community may see and respectfully adore the Body and Blood of Christ.

Kneeling

This is a common way to show respect and to worship.

23

We say the Lord's Prayer

Jesus has taught us that God is the Father of all human beings and that we can call upon God at any time. Together we recite or sing this prayer.

Priest: At the Saviour's command and formed by divine teaching, we dare to say:

Everyone: Our Father,
who art in heaven,
hallowed be thy name;
thy kingdom come,
thy will be done
on earth as it is in heaven.
Give us this day our daily bread,
and forgive us our trespasses,
as we forgive those who trespass against us;
and lead us not into temptation,
but deliver us from evil.

Priest: Deliver us, Lord, we pray, from every evil, graciously grant peace in our days, that, by the help of your mercy, we may be always free from sin and safe from all distress, as we await the blessed hope and the coming of our Saviour, Jesus Christ.

Everyone: For the kingdom,
the power and the glory are yours
now and for ever.

What does it mean?

Saviour

This is one of the names we give to Jesus because he saves us from evil and death.

Heaven

Heaven is a special way of being with God after our life on earth is over.

Kingdom

Jesus speaks of God as king when he says: "The kingdom of God is at hand." With his life, Jesus shows us that God is present in our midst as a king who loves us. When we live as Jesus did, we welcome the kingdom of God.

Trespasses

These refer to our lack of love and to the sins we commit.

Temptation

This is a desire we sometimes feel to do things we know are wrong.

We share the peace of Christ

God is our Father and we are brothers and sisters in Christ.
In order to show that we are one family, the priest invites us to
offer each other a sign of peace.

Priest: Lord Jesus Christ, who said to your Apostles: Peace I
leave you, my peace I give you, look not on our sins,
but on the faith of your Church, and graciously grant
her peace and unity in accordance with your will.
Who live and reign for ever and ever.

Everyone: Amen.

Priest: The peace of the Lord be with you always.

Everyone: And with your spirit.

Priest: Let us offer each other the sign of peace.

*At this time, by a handshake, a hug or a bow,
we give to those near us a sign of Christ's peace.
Immediately after, we say:*

Everyone: Lamb of God, you take away the sins of the world,
have mercy on us.

   of God, you take away the sins of the world,
have mercy on us.

   of God, you take away the sins of the world,
grant us peace.

What does it mean?

Unity

When we get together each Sunday to celebrate the Lord's Supper, we recognize our unity, or oneness, since we are all children of the same loving Father.

Lamb of God

In the Old Testament, believers offered a lamb to God. We call Jesus the Lamb of God because he offers his life to God.

Gestures

The sign of peace

We shake hands, hug or bow to one another to share the peace that comes from Christ. It is a sign of our commitment to live in peace with others.

We receive Jesus in communion

When we receive communion, the Bread of life, we are fed with the life of Christ.

The priest breaks the host and says:

Priest: Behold the Lamb of God, behold him who takes away the sins of the world. Blessed are those called to the supper of the Lamb.

Everyone: Lord, I am not worthy that you should enter under my roof, but only say the word and my soul shall be healed.

It is time to come up to receive communion. The priest or the communion minister says:

Priest: The Body of Christ.

Everyone: Amen.

Some questions

Why do we go to communion?

When we eat the bread and drink the wine, we receive Jesus. He gives himself to us this way so we can live for God. Sharing the Body and Blood of Christ in communion creates among us a special 'one-ness' with God and with each other.

Why is the bread we share during Mass called a "host"?

The word host means "victim who is offered." The consecrated host is Jesus Christ, who offers himself in order to give life to others.

Gestures

The priest breaks the bread

The priest breaks the bread in the same way that Jesus did during the Last Supper, in order to share it. The early Christians used to call the Mass "the breaking of the bread."

Receiving the host

The priest or communion minister places the host in your open hand. You eat the bread carefully and return to your place. You take a few moments of quiet prayer to thank God for this Bread of life.

Sending Forth

The Lord sends us home

After announcements, the priest blesses us in the name of God. We are then sent to live out our faith among all the people we meet during the week.

Priest: The Lord be with you.

Everyone: And with your spirit.

Priest: May almighty God bless you, the Father, and the Son, and the Holy Spirit.

Everyone: Amen.

Then the priest sends us out, saying:

Priest: Go in peace, glorifying the Lord by your life.

Everyone: Thanks be to God.

What does it mean?

The word "Mass"

The word "Mass" comes from the second word in the Latin phrase that was once used by the priest to announce the end of the Sunday celebration: *Ite missa est* — Go forth, the Mass is ended.

Communion for the sick

Sometimes people who are sick cannot be present at Sunday Mass. Certain members of the parish, known as communion ministers, can take consecrated hosts to the homes of sick people so that they can receive communion and be assured that the rest of the community is praying for them.

Gesture

Blessing

The priest makes the sign of the cross over the people in church. With this blessing we are sent out with the loving strength of God to live a life of love and service to others.

Dismissal

We cannot stay together in the church all week. When the Mass is ended, we must go our separate ways, in peace and love, to witness to the risen Jesus in the world today.

Liturgical Year

The readings for Sunday Mass and feast days change according to the liturgical calendar.

What is the liturgical year?

Throughout the year, Christians celebrate together important moments in Jesus' life. This is the liturgical year. There are five seasons: Advent, Christmas, Lent, Easter and Ordinary Time.

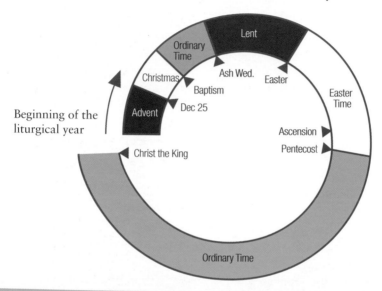

Advent is a time of waiting. It begins 4 weeks before Christmas. We prepare to welcome Jesus.

Christmas season celebrates the life of Jesus from his birth to his baptism. It includes Epiphany: Jesus welcomes the whole world.

During the 40 days of Lent — Ash Wednesday to Holy Saturday — we prepare for the great feast of Easter, the most important moment of the year.

Easter Time is a season to celebrate Jesus' victory over death. It lasts from Easter Sunday to Pentecost, when the Holy Spirit comes upon the disciples.

The season in green above is called Ordinary Time because the Sundays are arranged using 'ordinal numbers.' It recounts many of the things Jesus did and said during his lifetime.

1st Sunday of Advent

A reading from the book of the Prophet Jeremiah
(33.14-16)

The days are surely coming, says the Lord, when I will fulfill the promise I made to the house of Israel and the house of Judah.

In those days and at that time I will cause a righteous Branch to spring up for David; and he shall execute justice and righteousness in the land.

In those days Judah will be saved and Jerusalem will live in safety. And this is the name by which it will be called: "The Lord is our righteousness."

The word of the Lord. **Thanks be to God.**

Psalm 25

R̰ **To you, O Lord, I lift my soul.**

Make me to know your ways, O Lord,
teach me your paths.
Lead me in your truth and teach me,
for you are the God of my salvation. R̰

Good and upright is the Lord;
therefore he instructs sinners in the way.
He leads the humble in what is right,
and teaches the humble his way. R̰

All the paths of the Lord are steadfast love and faithfulness,
for those who keep his covenant and his decrees.
The friendship of the Lord is for those who fear him,
and he makes his covenant known to them. R̰

A reading from the first Letter of Saint Paul to the Thessalonians (3.12 – 4.2)

Brothers and sisters: May the Lord make you increase and abound in love for one another and for all, just as we abound in love for you. And may he so strengthen your hearts in holiness that you may be blameless before our God and Father at the coming of our Lord Jesus with all his saints.

Finally, brothers and sisters, we ask and urge you in the Lord Jesus that, as you learned from us how you ought to live and to please God, as, in fact, you are doing, you should do so more and more. For you know what instructions we gave you through the Lord Jesus.

The word of the Lord. **Thanks be to God.**

A reading from the holy Gospel according to Luke (21.25-28, 34-36)

Jesus spoke to his disciples: "There will be signs in the sun, the moon, and the stars and on the earth distress among nations confused by the roaring of the sea and the waves. People will faint from fear and foreboding of what is coming upon the world, for the powers of the heavens will be shaken.

"Then they will see 'the Son of Man coming in a cloud' with power and great glory. Now when these things begin to take place, stand up and raise your heads, because your redemption is drawing near.

"Be on guard so that your hearts are not weighed down with dissipation and drunkenness and the worries of this life, and that day catch you unexpectedly, like a trap. For it will come upon all who live on the face of the whole earth. Be alert at all times, praying that you may have the strength to escape all these things that will take place, and to stand before the Son of Man."

The Gospel of the Lord. **Praise to you, Lord Jesus Christ.**

With the season of Advent, which means 'coming,' we begin a new liturgical year. Advent lasts four weeks and during this time the liturgical colour is purple. Purple is the colour of waiting; it reminds us to prepare our hearts to celebrate the birth of Jesus at Christmas and his return at the end of time.

Jeremiah lived about 600 years before Jesus. When he was till a young boy, God called him to guide the people of Israel back to God. Many people ignored Jeremiah at first, and sent him away. But when the people of Israel feared that God had stopped loving them, Jeremiah gave them hope that God would not abandon them.

At the time of Jeremiah, God's people were divided into two kingdoms: the house of Israel in the north and the house of Judah in the south. Jeremiah announced God's wish for both kingdoms to be united into one nation, under one covenant.

A Branch for David is the family that is descended from David: his children and all who are born from them. When the prophet Jeremiah announced a new branch, he was speaking of the coming of the Messiah, the Christ.

Paul wrote two letters to the Thessalonians, Christians who lived in Thessalonica, in Greece. In this letter Paul praises them and encourages them to continue to love one another.

Jesus tells his friends to be alert at all times, ready to meet the Son of Man whenever he arrives. Advent is a time of waiting, and we too are called to be alert for the coming of Jesus in our lives.

December 9

2nd Sunday of Advent

Take off the garment of your sorrow and affliction, O Jerusalem,
and put on forever the beauty of the glory from God.
Put on the robe of the righteousness that comes from God;
put on your head the diadem of the glory of the Everlasting;
for God will show your splendour everywhere under heaven.
For God will give you evermore the name,
"Righteous Peace, Godly Glory."

Arise, O Jerusalem, stand upon the height;
look toward the east,
and see your children gathered from west and east
at the word of the Holy One,
rejoicing that God has remembered them.
For they went out from you on foot,
led away by their enemies;
but God will bring them back to you,
carried in glory, as on a royal throne.

For God has ordered that every high mountain
and the everlasting hills be made low
and the valleys filled up, to make level ground,
so that Israel may walk safely in the glory of God.
The woods and every fragrant tree
have shaded Israel at God's command.
For God will lead Israel with joy,
in the light of his glory,
with the mercy and righteousness that come from him.

The word of the Lord. **Thanks be to God.**

R. **The Lord has done great things for us;**
we are filled with joy.

When the Lord restored the fortunes of Zion,
we were like those who dream.
Then our mouth was filled with laughter,
and our tongue with shouts of joy. R.

Then it was said among the nations,
"The Lord has done great things for them."
The Lord has done great things for us,
and we rejoiced. R.

Restore our fortunes, O Lord,
like the watercourses in the desert of the Negev.
May those who sow in tears
reap with shouts of joy. R.

Those who go out weeping,
bearing the seed for sowing,
shall come home with shouts of joy,
carrying their sheaves. R.

A reading from the Letter of Saint Paul to the Philippians (1.3-6, 8-11)

Brothers and sisters, I thank my God every time I remember you, constantly praying with joy in every one of my prayers for all of you, because of your sharing in the Gospel from the first day until now.

I am confident of this, that the one who began a good work among you will bring it to completion by the day of Jesus Christ.

For God is my witness, how I long for all of you with the compassion of Christ Jesus. And this is my prayer, that your love may overflow more and more with knowledge and full insight to help you determine what is best, so that in the day of Christ you may be pure and blameless, having produced the harvest of righteousness that comes through Jesus Christ for the glory and praise of God.

The word of the Lord. **Thanks be to God.**

In the fifteenth year of the reign of Emperor Tiberius, when Pontius Pilate was governor of Judea, and Herod was ruler of Galilee, and his brother Philip ruler of the region of Ituraea and Trachonitis, and Lysanias ruler of Abilene, during the high priesthood of Annas and Caiaphas, the word of God came to John son of Zechariah in the wilderness.

He went into all the region around the Jordan, proclaiming a baptism of repentance for the forgiveness of sins, as it is written in the book of the words of the Prophet Isaiah, "The voice of one crying out in the wilderness: 'Prepare the way of the Lord, make his paths straight. Every valley shall be filled, and every mountain and hill shall be made low, and the crooked shall be made straight, and the rough ways made smooth; and all flesh shall see the salvation of God.'"

The Gospel of the Lord. **Praise to you, Lord Jesus Christ.**

The book of the Prophet Baruch was written about 200 years before Jesus was born. It tells the story of the people of Israel while they were forced to live in exile in Babylon. Baruch urges the people to follow God and stay faithful to him.

From west and east means from all across the world — similar to saying "from all the corners of the world." This statement reminds us that God desires all people to live in peace.

When he was in prison, Paul wrote a letter to the Philippians, a community of Christians in Philippi, Greece. He thanked them for their help and encouraged them to keep their faith in Jesus strong.

Knowledge and full insight are gifts from God. They help us know what God wants us to do.

Emperor Tiberius was a Roman emperor who ruled after Augustus Caesar. He ruled the Roman Empire during the time Jesus lived.

Pontius Pilate was appointed by the Romans to govern the area of Judea, the southern region of Israel. Jerusalem and Bethlehem were located in Judea.

Herod was the Jewish ruler of Galilee, an area in the north of Israel, during the time of Emperor Tiberius. Nazareth was located in Galilee; this is why Jesus was called a Galilean. The Herod mentioned in today's Gospel was the son of King Herod who ruled at the time of Jesus' birth.

A baptism of repentance is a sign that a person wants to turn back to God. John the Baptist baptized people in the River Jordan to show that their sins were washed away. Today, the sacrament of baptism unites us with Jesus and makes us part of the Church.

December 16

3rd Sunday of Advent

Sing aloud, O daughter Zion; shout, O Israel!
Rejoice and exult with all your heart,
O daughter of Jerusalem!
The Lord has taken away the judgments against you,
he has turned away your enemies.
The king of Israel, the Lord, is in your midst;
you shall fear disaster no more.

On that day it shall be said to Jerusalem:
Do not fear, O Zion;
do not let your hands grow weak.
The Lord, your God, is in your midst,
a warrior who gives victory;
he will rejoice over you with gladness,
he will renew you in his love.
The Lord, your God, will exult over you with loud singing
as on a day of festival.

The word of the Lord. **Thanks be to God.**

R. **Shout aloud and sing for joy:**
great in your midst is the Holy One of Israel.

Surely God is my salvation;
I will trust, and will not be afraid,
for the Lord God is my strength and my might;
he has become my salvation.
With joy you will draw water
from the wells of salvation. R.

Give thanks to the Lord,
call on his name;
make known his deeds among the nations;
proclaim that his name is exalted. R.

Sing praises to the Lord,
for he has done gloriously;
let this be known in all the earth.
Shout aloud and sing for joy, O royal Zion,
for great in your midst
is the Holy One of Israel. R.

A reading from the Letter of Saint Paul to the Philippians (4.4-7)

Rejoice in the Lord always; again I will say, Rejoice.

Let your gentleness be known to everyone. The Lord is near.
Do not worry about anything, but in everything by prayer and
supplication with thanksgiving let your requests be made known
to God.

And the peace of God, which surpasses all understanding, will
guard your hearts and your minds in Christ Jesus.

The word of the Lord. **Thanks be to God.**

The crowds, who were gathering to be baptized by John, asked him, "What should we do?" In reply John said to them, "Whoever has two coats must share with anyone who has none; and whoever has food must do likewise."

Even tax collectors came to be baptized, and they asked him, "Teacher, what should we do?" He said to them, "Collect no more than the amount prescribed for you." Soldiers also asked him, "And we, what should we do?" He said to them, "Do not extort money from anyone by threats or false accusation, and be satisfied with your wages."

As the people were filled with expectation, and all were questioning in their hearts concerning John, whether he might be the Messiah, John answered all of them by saying, "I baptize you with water; but one who is more powerful than I is coming; I am not worthy to untie the thong of his sandals. He will baptize you with the Holy Spirit and fire. His winnowing fork is in his hand, to clear his threshing floor and to gather the wheat into his granary; but the chaff he will burn with unquenchable fire."

So, with many other exhortations, John proclaimed the good news to the people.

The Gospel of the Lord. **Praise to you, Lord Jesus Christ.**

The prophet Zephaniah lived about 700 years before Jesus was born. The people of Israel had fallen away from their faith. Zephaniah tried to help them find their way back to God.

Zion was the name of a hill in Jerusalem, where the temple was built, but the city itself was often called Zion. Daughter Zion is another way of naming the entire nation, the whole people of God.

The Third Sunday of Advent is called "Gaudete" Sunday: *gaudete* is a Latin word for "Rejoice!" In today's readings, the Prophet Zephaniah, the Psalmist and Saint Paul all tell us to rejoice. Saint Paul tells the Philippians to rejoice and be happy because we all live in the Lord. Nothing can separate us from his love.

The Jewish people didn't like tax collectors because they worked for the Romans, who were foreigners ruling over Israel. Also, many tax collectors cheated people and took more money for taxes than they were supposed to.

To extort money is to force people to give money against their will. Jesus tells us always to be honest with others and treat everyone fairly.

A winnowing fork is a big wooden tool for separating the wheat, which is good to eat, from its husk, which is not edible. It separates the good from the bad.

4th Sunday of Advent

The Lord says to his people:
"You, O Bethlehem of Ephrathah,
who are one of the little clans of Judea,
from you shall come forth for me
one who is to rule in Israel,
whose origin is from of old, from ancient days."

Therefore he shall give them up until the time
when she who is in labour has brought forth;
then the rest of his kindred
shall return to the children of Israel.
And he shall stand and feed his flock
in the strength of the Lord,
in the majesty of the name of the Lord his God.

And they shall live secure,
for now he shall be great to the ends of the earth;
and he shall be peace.

The word of the Lord. **Thanks be to God.**

Psalm 80

R. **Restore us, O God;**
let your face shine, that we may be saved.

Give ear, O Shepherd of Israel,
you who are enthroned upon the cherubim, shine forth.
Stir up your might,
and come to save us. R.

Turn again, O God of hosts;
look down from heaven, and see;
have regard for this vine,
the stock that your right hand has planted. R.

But let your hand be upon the man at your right,
the son of man you have made strong for yourself.
Then we will never turn back from you;
give us life, and we will call on your name. R.

Brothers and sisters: When Christ came into the world, he said, "Sacrifices and offerings you have not desired, but a body you have prepared for me; in burnt offerings and sin offerings you have taken no pleasure. Then I said, as it is written of me in the scroll of the book, 'See, God, I have come to do your will, O God.'"

When Christ said, "You have neither desired nor taken pleasure in sacrifices and offerings and burnt offerings and sin offerings" (these are offered according to the Law), then he added, "See, I have come to do your will." He abolishes the first in order to establish the second.

And it is by God's will that we have been sanctified through the offering of the body of Jesus Christ once for all.

The word of the Lord. **Thanks be to God.**

Mary set out and went with haste to a Judean town in the hill country, where she entered the house of Zechariah and greeted Elizabeth.

When Elizabeth heard Mary's greeting, the child leaped in her womb. And Elizabeth was filled with the Holy Spirit and exclaimed with a loud cry, "Blessed

are you among women, and blessed is the fruit of your womb. And why has this happened to me, that the mother of my Lord comes to me? For as soon as I heard the sound of your greeting, the child in my womb leaped for joy. And blessed is she who believed that there would be a fulfillment of what was spoken to her by the Lord."

The Gospel of the Lord.
Praise to you, Lord Jesus Christ.

49

Micah was a prophet who lived about 700 years before Jesus was born. It was a hard time for Israel. The Assyrians were taking over and the Israelites were not working together or helping the poor. Micah told them God was angry with them, but there was hope: if they changed their ways, things would get better.

Bethlehem is the city of King David, one of Jesus' ancestors. It is a few kilometres south of Jerusalem, in Judea. Jesus was born there. (See the map on page 328.)

Jesus came to do God's will: what God wanted him to do or make happen. When we pray the "Our Father," we say to God, "Thy will be done." God's will was to save us from sin and bring us peace through Jesus. We are also to do God's will: to help build his kingdom of peace.

Mary was an ordinary person who was asked to do an extraordinary thing. God asked Mary, who was engaged to be married to Joseph, to be the mother of his son, Jesus. She said yes. We are thankful for Mary's generosity because, through her son Jesus, we have eternal life. Since Jesus is our brother, Mary is also our mother. She listens to our prayers and presents them to Jesus for us.

Elizabeth, Mary's cousin, became pregnant at an age when women can no longer have children. Her husband, Zechariah, was a priest of the temple in Jerusalem. Their son, John the Baptist, Jesus' cousin, was six months older than Jesus.

Blessed are you among women. With these words of praise, Elizabeth tells Mary that she is special to God. Mary is the best example of discipleship for Christians of all ages, because she said "yes" to God. Elizabeth's words to Mary are part of the prayer "Hail Mary."

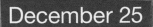
December 25

The Nativity of the Lord
Christmas

The people who walked in darkness have seen a great light;
those who lived in a land of deep darkness —
on them light has shone.
You have multiplied the nation,
you have increased its joy;
they rejoice before you
as with joy at the harvest,
as people exult when dividing plunder.

For the yoke of their burden,
and the bar across their shoulders,
the rod of their oppressor,
you have broken as on the day of Midian.

For a child has been born for us,
a son given to us;
authority rests upon his shoulders;
and he is named
Wonderful Counsellor, Mighty God,
Everlasting Father, Prince of Peace.

His authority shall grow continually,
and there shall be endless peace
for the throne of David and his kingdom.
He will establish and uphold it
with justice and with righteousness
from this time onward and forevermore.
The zeal of the Lord of hosts will do this.

The word of the Lord. **Thanks be to God.**

R. **Today is born our Saviour, Christ the Lord.**

O sing to the Lord a new song;
sing to the Lord, all the earth.
Sing to the Lord, bless his name;
tell of his salvation from day to day. R.

Declare his glory among the nations,
his marvellous works among all the peoples.
For great is the Lord, and greatly to be praised;
he is to be revered above all gods. R.

Let the heavens be glad, and let the earth rejoice;
let the sea roar, and all that fills it;
let the field exult, and everything in it.
Then shall all the trees of the forest sing for joy. R.

Rejoice before the Lord; for he is coming,
for he is coming to judge the earth.
He will judge the world with righteousness,
and the peoples with his truth. R.

A reading from the Letter of Saint Paul to Titus
(2.11-14)

Beloved: The grace of God has appeared, bringing salvation to all, training us to renounce impiety and worldly passions, and in the present age to live lives that are self-controlled, upright, and godly, while we wait for the blessed hope and the manifestation of the glory of our great God and Saviour, Jesus Christ.

He it is who gave himself for us that he might redeem us from all iniquity and purify for himself a people of his own who are zealous for good deeds.

The word of the Lord. **Thanks be to God.**

A reading from the holy Gospel according to Luke
(2.1-16)

In those days a decree went out from Caesar Augustus that all the world should be registered. This was the first registration and was taken while Quirinius was governor of Syria. All went to their own towns to be registered. Joseph also went from the town of Nazareth in Galilee to Judea, to the city of David called Bethlehem, because he was descended from the house and family of David. He went to be registered with Mary, to whom he was engaged and who was expecting a child.

While they were there, the time came for her to deliver her child. And she gave birth to her firstborn son and wrapped him in swaddling clothes, and laid him in a manger, because there was no place for them in the inn.

In that region there were shepherds living in the fields, keeping watch over their flock by night. Then an Angel of the Lord stood before them, and the glory of the Lord shone around them, and they were terrified. But the Angel said to them, "Do not be afraid; for see — I am bringing you good news of great joy for all the people: to you is born this day in the city of David a Saviour, who is the Christ, the Lord. This will be a sign for you: you will find a child wrapped in swaddling clothes and lying in a manger."

And suddenly there was with the Angel a multitude of the heavenly host, praising God and saying, "Glory to God in the highest heaven, and on earth peace among those whom he favours!"

When the Angels had left them and gone into heaven, the shepherds said to one another, "Let us go now to Bethlehem and see this thing that has taken place, which the Lord has made known to us." So they went with haste and found Mary and Joseph, and the child lying in the manger.

The Gospel of the Lord. **Praise to you, Lord Jesus Christ.**

Christmas Day is celebrated on December 25th, but the Christmas season lasts for three weeks, ending with the Baptism of Jesus in January. The liturgical colour for this season is white, the colour of joy and celebration.

Prophets like Isaiah were good men and women who spoke for God. Sometimes their messages were demanding: they asked people to change their lives and attitudes to grow closer to God. At other times, they brought words of comfort.

We sing for joy because our hearts are full of happiness: God has come to be with his people. In today's psalm, we see that all creation — even the trees! — rejoice and glory in the Lord.

A manger is a wooden crate filled with hay to feed the animals in a stable. The baby Jesus was placed in a manger soon after he was born. It is amazing that God would choose to be born in such a simple place.

An Angel of the Lord is a messenger of God. Angels appear many times in the Bible, as we see angels revealing God's plan in the lives of Jesus, Mary and Joseph.

Merry Christmas!

Glory to God in the highest and on earth peace to all people!

In due time Hannah conceived and bore a son. She named him Samuel, for she said, "I have asked him of the Lord." Elkanah and all his household went up to offer to the Lord the yearly sacrifice, and to pay his vow. But Hannah did not go up, for she said to her husband, "As soon as the child is weaned, I will bring him, that he may appear in the presence of the Lord, and remain there forever; I will offer him as a nazirite for all time."

When she had weaned him, she took him up with her, along with a three-year-old bull, a measure of flour, and a skin of wine. She brought him to the house of the Lord at Shiloh; and the child was young. Then they slaughtered the bull, and they brought the child to Eli. And she said, "Oh, my lord! As you live, my lord, I am the woman who was standing here in your presence, praying to the Lord. For this child I prayed; and the Lord has granted me the petition that I made to him. Therefore I have lent him to the Lord; as long as he lives, he is given to the Lord." She left him there for the Lord.

The word of the Lord. **Thanks be to God.**

Psalm 84

R⁓ **Blessed are those who live in your house, O Lord.**

How lovely is your dwelling place,
O Lord of hosts!
My soul longs, indeed it faints for the courts of the Lord;
my heart and my flesh sing for joy to the living God. R⁓

Blessed are those who live in your house,
ever singing your praise.
Blessed are those whose strength is in you,
in whose heart are the highways to Zion. R⁓

O Lord God of hosts, hear my prayer;
give ear, O God of Jacob!
Behold our shield, O God;
look on the face of your anointed. R⁓

For a day in your courts is better
than a thousand elsewhere.
I would rather be a doorkeeper in the house of my God
than live in the tents of wickedness. R⁓

A reading from the first Letter of Saint John
(3.1-2, 21-24)

Beloved: See what love the Father has given us, that we should be called children of God; and that is what we are. The reason the world does not know us is that it did not know him. Beloved, we are God's children now; what we will be has not yet been revealed. What we do know is this: when he is revealed, we will be like him, for we will see him as he is.

Beloved, if our hearts do not condemn us, we have boldness before God; and we receive from him whatever we ask, because we obey his commandments and do what pleases him. And this is his commandment, that we should believe in the name of his Son Jesus Christ and love one another, just as he has commanded us. Whoever obeys his commandments abides in him, and he abides in them. And by this we know that he abides in us, by the Spirit that he has given us.

The word of the Lord. **Thanks be to God.**

A reading from the holy Gospel according to Luke
(2.41-52)

Every year the parents of Jesus went to Jerusalem for the festival of the Passover. And when he was twelve years old, they went up as usual for the festival.

When the festival was ended and they started to return, the boy Jesus stayed behind in Jerusalem, but his parents did not know it. Assuming that he was in the group of travellers, they went a day's journey. Then they started to look for him among their relatives and friends. When they did not find him, they returned to Jerusalem to search for him.

After three days they found him in the temple, sitting among the teachers, listening to them and asking them questions. And all who heard him were amazed at his understanding and his answers. When his parents saw him they were astonished; and his mother said to him, "Child, why have you treated us like this? Look, your father and I have been searching for you in great anxiety." He said to them, "Why were you searching for me? Did you not know that I must be in my Father's house?" But they did not understand what he said to them.

Then he went down with them and came to Nazareth, and was obedient to them. His mother treasured all these things in her heart. And Jesus increased in wisdom and in years, and in favour with God and human beings.

The Gospel of the Lord. **Praise to you, Lord Jesus Christ.**

Like the Holy Family of Mary, Joseph and Jesus, our family is a gift from God. We take care of this gift and treasure it when we share our lives, listen to one another and pray together.

Samuel, a prophet and judge in Israel, was born over 1,000 years before Jesus. The Lord chose Samuel to anoint Saul, the first king of Israel. He also anointed David, who was king after Saul. The Bible contains two books in his name: 1 Samuel and 2 Samuel.

A nazirite was a person who lived a special life of holiness. In Samuel's case, his mother Hannah had longed for a child but was barren. She promised God that if God gave her a son, she would offer him to God in this special way, as a nazirite. God heard and answered her prayer.

Eli was the chief priest at the sanctuary at Shiloh (pronounced 'shy-low'). His task was to guard the sanctuary, especially the Ark of the Covenant that was kept there.

In this reading, the world refers to people who think only about things like money and having fun. Worldly people often find it difficult to make room in their hearts for Jesus.

The teachers in the temple were men who spent their lives studying the Bible and sharing their knowledge with the people. They were wise and highly respected, and not the usual companions for a child.

January 1

Solemnity of Mary, the Holy Mother of God

A reading from the book of Numbers (6.22-27)

The Lord spoke to Moses: Speak to Aaron and his sons, saying,
Thus you shall bless the children of Israel: You shall say to them,

The Lord bless you and keep you;
the Lord make his face to shine upon you, and be gracious to you;
the Lord lift up his countenance upon you, and give you peace.

So they shall put my name on the children of Israel,
and I will bless them.

The word of the Lord. **Thanks be to God.**

Psalm 67

R̰ **May God be gracious to us and bless us.**

May God be gracious to us and bless us
and make his face to shine upon us,
that your way may be known upon earth,
your saving power among all nations. R̰

Let the nations be glad and sing for joy,
for you judge the peoples with equity
and guide the nations upon earth.
Let the peoples praise you, O God;
let all the peoples praise you. R̰

The earth has yielded its increase;
God, our God, has blessed us.
May God continue to bless us;
let all the ends of the earth revere him. R̰

A reading from the Letter of Saint Paul to the Galatians (4.4-7)

Brothers and sisters: When the fullness of time had come, God sent his Son, born of a woman, born under the law, in order to redeem those who were under the law, so that we might receive adoption to sonship.

And because you are sons and daughters, God has sent the Spirit of his Son into our hearts, crying, "Abba! Father!" So you are no longer slave but son, and if son then also heir, through God.

The word of the Lord. **Thanks be to God.**

A reading from the holy Gospel according to Luke (2.16-21)

The shepherds went with haste to Bethlehem and found Mary and Joseph, and the child lying in the manger. When they saw this, they made known what had been told them about this child; and all who heard it were amazed at what the shepherds told them.

But Mary treasured all these words and pondered them in her heart.

The shepherds returned, glorifying and praising God for all they had heard and seen, as it had been told them.

After eight days had passed, it was time to circumcise the child; and he was called Jesus, the name given by the Angel before he was conceived in the womb.

The Gospel of the Lord.
Praise to you, Lord Jesus Christ.

The book of Numbers is found in the Hebrew Scriptures or Old Testament. It is called "Numbers" because it talks about many numbers and times when the people of Israel were counted. In Hebrew, it is called "In the Desert," because it tells of the travels of the Israelites, after they left slavery in Egypt.

Moses was a friend of God who was born in Egypt when the Israelites were slaves there. When God asked him to lead the people to freedom, Moses said yes because he loved God and didn't want the people to suffer any more. The people left Egypt on a journey called the "Exodus" about 1,250 years before the time of Jesus.

Aaron, Moses' older brother, helped him free the Israelites. When Moses went up Mount Sinai to receive God's law, Aaron stayed with the people.

Children of Israel is the name of the people God chose to help everyone in the world know God's love.

To judge with equity is to be fair to everyone. In the Psalm, the Psalmist is praising God for God's fairness to all people on earth.

Fullness of time means when the time was right for God to send Jesus into the world.

In Aramaic, the language Jesus spoke, Abba means "Daddy." By calling God "Abba," Jesus shows that we can talk to God with the same trust and love that small children have for their father.

A manger is the place in a barn or stable for the animals' food. Its name is from the French word *manger*, to eat.

To ponder means to think about something a lot. Like all mothers, Mary remembered all the details surrounding the birth of her child.

January 6

Epiphany of the Lord

Arise, shine, for your light has come,
and the glory of the Lord has risen upon you!
For darkness shall cover the earth,
and thick darkness the peoples;
but the Lord will arise upon you,
and his glory will appear over you.
Nations shall come to your light,
and kings to the brightness of your dawn.
Lift up your eyes and look around;
they all gather together, they come to you;
your sons shall come from far away,
and your daughters shall be carried on their nurses' arms.

Then you shall see and be radiant;
your heart shall thrill and rejoice,
because the abundance of the sea shall be brought to you,
the wealth of the nations shall come to you.
A multitude of camels shall cover you,
the young camels of Midian and Ephah;
all those from Sheba shall come.
They shall bring gold and frankincense,
and shall proclaim the praise of the Lord.

The word of the Lord. **Thanks be to God.**

R. **Lord, every nation on earth will adore you.**

Give the king your justice, O God,
and your righteousness to a king's son.
May he judge your people with righteousness,
and your poor with justice. R.

In his days may righteousness flourish
and peace abound, until the moon is no more.
May he have dominion from sea to sea,
and from the River to the ends of the earth. R.

May the kings of Tarshish and of the isles render him tribute,
may the kings of Sheba and Seba bring gifts.
May all kings fall down before him,
all nations give him service. R.

For he delivers the needy one who calls,
the poor and the one who has no helper.
He has pity on the weak and the needy,
and saves the lives of the needy. R.

A reading from the Letter of Saint Paul to the Ephesians (3.2-3, 5-6)

Brothers and sisters: Surely you have already heard of the commission of God's grace that was given me for you, and how the mystery was made known to me by revelation.

In former generations this mystery was not made known to humankind as it has now been revealed to his holy Apostles and Prophets by the Spirit: that is, the Gentiles have become fellow heirs, members of the same body, and sharers in the promise in Christ Jesus through the Gospel.

The word of the Lord. **Thanks be to God.**

In the time of King Herod, after Jesus was born in Bethlehem of Judea, wise men from the East came to Jerusalem, asking, "Where is the child who has been born king of the Jews? For we observed his star at its rising, and have come to pay him homage."

When King Herod heard this, he was frightened, and all Jerusalem with him; and calling together all the chief priests and scribes of the people, he inquired of them where the Messiah was to be born. They told him, "In Bethlehem of Judea; for so it has been written by the Prophet: 'And you, Bethlehem, in the land of Judah, are by no means least among the rulers of Judah; for from you shall come a ruler who is to shepherd my people Israel.'"

Then Herod secretly called for the wise men and learned from them the exact time when the star had appeared. Then he sent them to Bethlehem, saying, "Go and search diligently for the child; and when you have found him, bring me word so that I may also go and pay him homage."

When they had heard the king, they set out; and there, ahead of them, went the star that they had seen at its rising, until it stopped over the place where the child was. When they saw that the star had stopped, they were overwhelmed with joy.

On entering the house, they saw the child with Mary his mother; and they knelt down and paid him homage. Then, opening their treasure chests, they offered him gifts of gold, frankincense, and myrrh.

And having been warned in a dream not to return to Herod, they left for their own country by another road.

The Gospel of the Lord.
Praise to you, Lord Jesus Christ.

Epiphany is a Greek word that means "unveiling," where something is revealed. God revealed his love for all people by sending us his Son, Jesus, as a baby.

Midian, Ephah and Sheba were three ancient kingdoms near Israel. In the book of the Prophet Isaiah in the Bible, they represent all the nations outside Israel.

The Ephesians were a group of Christians in the city of Ephesus. A letter Saint Paul wrote to them is now part of the Bible. Ephesus is located in modern-day Turkey.

A mystery is something that is very hard to understand. In Saint Paul's letter to the Ephesians, it means God's plan to create a human community in Christ.

To know something by revelation means that God has shown or given someone this knowledge.

Bethlehem of Judea is the city of King David, one of Jesus' ancestors. Joseph and Mary went to Bethlehem for a census (an official counting of all the people). Jesus was born during their stay there. See the map on page 328.

To pay someone homage is to show your respect or honour for them in a public way, such as by bowing or bringing gifts.

Messiah is an Aramaic word meaning "anointed." The chosen person was blessed with holy oil and given a special mission. The Greek word for "anointed" is "Christ."

Gold, frankincense and myrrh were three very expensive gifts: gold is a precious metal; frankincense and myrrh are rare, sweet-smelling incenses. Myrrh is the main ingredient in holy anointing oil.

January 13

Baptism of the Lord

A reading from the book of the Prophet Isaiah

(40.1-5, 9-11)

Comfort, O comfort my people,
says your God.
Speak tenderly to Jerusalem,
and cry to her
that she has served her term,
that her penalty is paid,
that she has received from the Lord's hand
double for all her sins.

A voice cries out:
"In the wilderness prepare the way of the Lord,
make straight in the desert a highway for our God.
Every valley shall be lifted up,
and every mountain and hill be made low;
the uneven ground shall become level,
and the rough places a plain.
Then the glory of the Lord shall be revealed,
and all people shall see it together,
for the mouth of the Lord has spoken."

Get you up to a high mountain,
O Zion, herald of good tidings;
lift up your voice with strength,
O Jerusalem, herald of good tidings,
lift it up, do not fear;
say to the cities of Judah,
"Here is your God!"

See, the Lord God comes with might,
and his arm rules for him;
his reward is with him,
and his recompense before him.
He will feed his flock like a shepherd;
he will gather the lambs in his arms,
and carry them in his bosom,
and gently lead the mother sheep.

The word of the Lord. **Thanks be to God.**

R̝ O bless the Lord, my soul!

O Lord my God, you are very great.
You are clothed with honour and majesty,
wrapped in light as with a garment.
You stretch out the heavens like a tent. R̝

You set the beams of your dwelling place on the waters,
you make the clouds your chariot,
you ride on the wings of the wind,
you make the winds your messengers,
fire and flame your ministers. R̝

O Lord, how manifold are your works!
In wisdom you have made them all;
the earth is full of your creatures.
Yonder is the sea, great and wide,
creeping things innumerable are there,
living things both small and great. R̝

Living things all look to you
to give them their food in due season;
when you give to them, they gather it up;
when you open your hand, they are filled with good things. R̝

When you take away their breath,
they die and return to their dust.
When you send forth your spirit, they are created;
and you renew the face of the earth. R̝

A reading from the Letter of Saint Paul to Titus
(2.11-14; 3.4-7)

Beloved: The grace of God has appeared, bringing salvation to all, training us to renounce impiety and worldly passions, and in the present age to live lives that are self-controlled, upright, and godly, while we wait for the blessed hope and the manifestation of the glory of our great God and Saviour, Jesus Christ.

He it is who gave himself for us that he might redeem us from all iniquity and purify for himself a people of his own who are zealous for good deeds.

For when the goodness and loving kindness of God our Saviour appeared, he saved us, not because of any works of righteousness that we had done, but according to his mercy, through the water of rebirth and renewal by the Holy Spirit. This Spirit he poured out on us richly through Jesus Christ our Saviour, so that, having been justified by his grace, we might become heirs according to the hope of eternal life.

The word of the Lord. **Thanks be to God.**

A reading from the holy Gospel according to Luke
(3.15-16, 21-22)

As the people were filled with expectation, and all were questioning in their hearts concerning John, whether he might be the Messiah, John answered all of them by saying, "I baptize you with water; but one who is more powerful than I is coming; I am not worthy to untie the thong of his sandals. He will baptize you with the Holy Spirit and fire."

Now when all the people were baptized, and when Jesus also had been baptized and was praying, the heaven was opened, and the Holy Spirit descended upon him in bodily form like a dove. And a voice came from heaven, "You are my Son, the Beloved; with you I am well pleased."

The Gospel of the Lord. **Praise to you, Lord Jesus Christ.**

Judah was one of the twelve sons of Jacob. Each son was the chief of one of the twelve tribes of Israel. The tribe of Judah established itself to the south of Jerusalem. In the first reading today Isaiah speaks of the citizens of Judah in reference to all the Israelites, not just those who lived in the region of Judah.

The Bible explains the great love of God (the shepherd) for us (the sheep). The shepherd cares for the sheep all day and night, and finds pastures where they have plenty to eat and drink.

The worldly passions arise when we live as if the most important thing in life is to please only ourselves. If this world were all there is, and if Jesus did not plan that we live as God's children, we might live as if God did not exist.

Saint Paul taught that we who are Jesus' friends should live without the need for so many things — we should live in a self-controlled manner. To be self-controlled is to eat, drink, talk, behave and enjoy ourselves in moderation.

Mercy is God's caress. God cares for everybody, especially for the poor and the little ones. Jesus asks us also to show God's mercy towards others.

Baptism brings us to renewal. It allows us to be "born" in a new way, united with the resurrected Jesus, among the great family of Christians which is the Church.

John the Baptist was the son of Zechariah and Elizabeth, who was a cousin of the Virgin Mary. He was known as "the precursor" because he preached that the Messiah was about to arrive. He was called John the Baptist because those who were converted by his preaching were baptized in order to prepare themselves for the coming of the Saviour.

When today's Gospel tells us that a voice from the sky said, "with you I am well pleased," this is showing us that Jesus is the Son of God and has God's approval. Jesus came to teach us the way we should live as brothers and sisters — as children of God.

2nd Sunday in Ordinary Time

A reading from the book of the Prophet Isaiah (62.1-5)

For Zion's sake I will not keep silent, and for Jerusalem's sake I will not rest, until her vindication shines out like the dawn, and her salvation like a burning torch.

The nations shall see your vindication, and all the kings your glory; and you shall be called by a new name that the mouth of the Lord will give. You shall be a crown of beauty in the hand of the Lord, and a royal diadem in the hand of your God.

You shall no more be termed Forsaken, and your land shall no more be termed Desolate; but you shall be called My Delight Is in Her, and your land Married; for the Lord delights in you, and your land shall be married.

For as a young man marries a young woman, so shall your builder marry you, and as the bridegroom rejoices over the bride, so shall your God rejoice over you.

The word of the Lord. **Thanks be to God.**

Psalm 96

R. **Declare the marvellous works of the Lord among all the peoples.**

O sing to the Lord a new song;
sing to the Lord, all the earth.
Sing to the Lord, bless his name;
tell of his salvation from day to day. R.

Declare his glory among the nations,
his marvellous works among all the peoples.
For great is the Lord, and greatly to be praised;
he is to be revered above all gods. R.

Ascribe to the Lord, O families of the peoples,
ascribe to the Lord glory and strength.
Ascribe to the Lord the glory due his name;
bring an offering, and come into his courts. R.

Worship the Lord in holy splendour;
tremble before him, all the earth.
Say among the nations, "The Lord is king!
He will judge the peoples with equity." R.

A reading from the first Letter of Saint Paul to the Corinthians (12.4-11)

Brothers and sisters: There are varieties of gifts, but the same Spirit; and there are varieties of services, but the same Lord; and there are varieties of activities, but it is the same God who activates all of them in everyone.

To each is given the manifestation of the Spirit for the common good. To one is given through the Spirit the utterance of wisdom, and to another the utterance of knowledge according to the same Spirit, to another faith by the same Spirit, to another gifts of healing by the one Spirit, to another the working of miracles, to another prophecy, to another the discernment of spirits, to another various kinds of tongues, to another the interpretation of tongues.

All these are activated by one and the same Spirit, who allots to each one individually just as the Spirit chooses.

The word of the Lord. **Thanks be to God.**

A reading from the holy Gospel according to John (2.1-12)

On the third day there was a wedding in Cana of Galilee, and the mother of Jesus was there. Jesus and his disciples had also been invited to the wedding.

When the wine gave out, the mother of Jesus said to him, "They have no wine." And Jesus said to her, "Woman, what concern is that to you and to me? My hour has not yet come." His mother said to the servants, "Do whatever he tells you."

Now standing there were six stone water jars for the Jewish rites of purification, each holding about a hundred litres. Jesus said to the servants, "Fill the jars with water." And they filled them up to the brim. He said to them, "Now draw some out, and take it to the chief steward." So they took it.

When the steward tasted the water that had become wine, and did not know where it came from (though the servants who had drawn the water knew), the steward called the bridegroom and said to him, "Everyone serves the good wine first, and then the inferior wine after the guests have become drunk. But you have kept the good wine until now."

Jesus did this, the first of his signs, in Cana of Galilee, and revealed his glory; and his disciples believed in him. After this he went down to Capernaum with his mother, his brothers, and his disciples; and they remained there a few days.

The Gospel of the Lord. **Praise to you, Lord Jesus Christ.**

KEY WORDS

Zion is the name of the ancient fort of Jerusalem, built on a hill. It is a way to refer to the entire city of Jerusalem.

When someone is called by a new name, we recognize that this person has changed for the better or is like a new person. The new name celebrates this change.

In the reading from Isaiah, the word married is used to describe the deep love that God has for his people. God's love is greater than human love and impossible to understand completely. Isaiah uses the love we feel for the person we marry as a way to help us understand God's love for us.

The Corinthians were members of a Christian community in Corinth that received several letters from Saint Paul. Corinth was the capital city of a Roman province in what is now Greece.

Saint Paul uses the word gifts to signify the qualities or skills that God gives to us. No two people are alike, and all our gifts are different. Yet we all receive our gifts from the Spirit and are called to use our gifts for the good of the community.

The Holy Spirit is the power of God that is present in our lives. There are three persons in God: God the Father, Jesus the Son, and the Holy Spirit. Jesus sent us his Spirit after he rose from the dead, to guide us and give us strength in following him.

Cana of Galilee is a town located near Nazareth. Jesus grew up in Nazareth, and when he went to Jerusalem people could tell he was from Galilee because of his accent and the way he spoke.

In John's Gospel, the miracles of Jesus are called signs — wonders he performed in order to encourage people to believe he was the one sent by God to save us.

3rd Sunday in Ordinary Time

The priest Ezra brought the Law before the assembly, both men and women and all who could hear with understanding. This was on the first day of the seventh month. He read from it facing the square before the Water Gate from early morning until midday, in the presence of the men and the women and those who could understand; and the ears of all the people were attentive to the book of the Law. The scribe Ezra stood on a wooden platform that had been made for the purpose.

And Ezra opened the book in the sight of all the people, for he was standing above all the people; and when he opened it, all the people stood up. Then Ezra blessed the Lord, the great God, and all the people answered, "Amen, Amen," lifting up their hands. Then they bowed their heads and worshipped the Lord with their faces to the ground.

So the Levites read from the book, from the Law of God, with interpretation. They gave the sense, so that the people understood the reading. And Nehemiah, who was the governor, and Ezra the priest and scribe, and the Levites who taught the people said to all the people, "This day is holy to the Lord your God; do not mourn or weep." For all the people wept when they heard the words of the Law.

Then Ezra said to them, "Go your way, eat the fat and drink sweet wine and send portions of them to those for whom nothing is prepared, for this day is holy to our Lord; and do not be grieved, for the joy of the Lord is your strength."

The word of the Lord. **Thanks be to God.**

R. **Your words, Lord, are spirit and life.**

The law of the Lord is perfect,
reviving the soul;
the decrees of the Lord are sure,
making wise the simple. R.

The precepts of the Lord are right,
rejoicing the heart;
the commandment of the Lord is clear,
enlightening the eyes. R.

The fear of the Lord is pure,
enduring forever;
the ordinances of the Lord are true
and righteous altogether. R.

Let the words of my mouth
and the meditation of my heart
be acceptable to you,
O Lord, my rock and my redeemer. R.

A reading from the first Letter of Saint Paul to the Corinthians (12.12-30)

For the shorter version, omit the indented parts.

Brothers and sisters: Just as the body is one and has many members, and all the members of the body, though many, are one body, so it is with Christ. For in the one Spirit we were all baptized into one body — Jews or Greeks, slaves or free — and we were all made to drink of one Spirit. Indeed, the body does not consist of one member but of many.

If the foot would say, "Because I am not a hand, I do not belong to the body," that would not make it any less a part of the body. And if the ear would say, "Because I am not an eye, I do not belong to the body," that would not make it any less a part of the body. If the whole body were an eye, where would the hearing be? If the whole body were hearing, where would the sense of smell be?

But as it is, God arranged the members in the body, each one of them, as he chose. If all were a single member, where would the body be? As it is, there are many members, yet one body. The eye cannot say to the hand, "I have no need of you," nor again the head to the feet, "I have no need of you." On the contrary, the members of the body that seem to be weaker are indispensable, and those members of the body that we think less honourable we clothe with greater honour, and our less respectable members are treated with greater respect; whereas our more respectable members do not need this.

But God has so arranged the body, giving the greater honour to the inferior member, that there may be no dissension within the body, but the members may have the same care for one another. If one member suffers, all suffer together with it; if one member is honoured, all rejoice together with it.

Now you are the body of Christ and individually members of it.

And God has appointed in the Church first Apostles, second Prophets, third Teachers; then deeds of power, then gifts of healing, forms of assistance, forms of leadership, various kinds of tongues.

Are all Apostles? Are all Prophets? Are all Teachers? Do all work miracles? Do all possess gifts of healing? Do all speak in tongues? Do all interpret?

The word of the Lord. **Thanks be to God.**

A reading from the holy Gospel according to Luke
(1.1-4; 4.14-21)

Since many have undertaken to set down an orderly account of the events that have been fulfilled among us, just as they were handed on to us by those who from the beginning were eyewitnesses and servants of the word, I too decided, after investigating everything carefully from the very first, to write an orderly account for you, most excellent Theophilus, so that you may know the truth concerning the things about which you have been instructed.

Jesus, filled with the power of the Spirit, returned to Galilee, and a report about him spread through all the surrounding country. He began to teach in their synagogues and was praised by everyone. When he came to Nazareth, where he had been brought up, he went to the synagogue on the Sabbath day, as was his custom.

He stood up to read, and the scroll of the Prophet Isaiah was given to him. He unrolled the scroll and found the place where it was written: "The Spirit of the Lord is upon me, because he has anointed me to bring good news to the poor. He has sent me to proclaim release to the captives and recovery of sight to the blind, to let the oppressed go free, to proclaim the year of the Lord's favour."

And he rolled up the scroll, gave it back to the attendant, and sat down. The eyes of all in the synagogue were fixed on him.

Then he began to say to them, "Today this Scripture has been fulfilled in your hearing."

The Gospel of the Lord. **Praise to you, Lord Jesus Christ.**

Ezra was a holy priest who, together with Nehemiah, encouraged the people to rebuild the city of Jerusalem 515 years before the birth of Christ. He also urged the people to respect the holy scriptures and to recommit themselves to their Covenant with God.

Amen is the Hebrew word meaning "yes," "I agree," "I promise." When we say it twice, we are emphasizing our agreement — we really mean what we say.

Saint Paul compares the Church to a body. Christ is the head, and we the people are the body of Christ. By this comparison we understand that Christ is most important; but just as the head needs the body, so we are all important to the life of the Church.

Theophilus literally means "friend or beloved of God" in Greek. This person was a representative of the Christian communities of Greece. Saint Luke addressed his Gospel as well as the Acts of the Apostles to him.

Synagogues are buildings that serve as meeting places for the Jewish community to pray and read the Scriptures together. They are like the temples or churches in other faiths.

Just as Christians gather together on Sunday for Mass, so the Jews gather to pray on the Sabbath Day, the seventh day, Saturday.

When someone is anointed, it is a sign that they have been given an important mission for the good of the community. Oil is rubbed on that person's forehead, hands or another part of the body. We are anointed when we are baptized and confirmed; a priest is anointed when he is ordained to the priesthood; and we are anointed when we receive the sacrament of the sick.

4th Sunday in Ordinary Time

A reading from the book of the Prophet Jeremiah
(1.4-5, 17-19)

The word of the Lord came to me saying, "Before I formed you in the womb I knew you, and before you were born I consecrated you; I appointed you a Prophet to the nations.

"Therefore, gird up your loins; stand up and tell the people everything that I command you. Do not break down before them, or I will break you before them. And I for my part have made you today a fortified city, an iron pillar, and a bronze wall, against the whole land — against the kings of Judah, its princes, its priests, and the people of the land.

"They will fight against you; but they shall not prevail against you, for I am with you, says the Lord, to deliver you."

The word of the Lord. **Thanks be to God.**

Psalm 71

R̰ **My mouth will tell, O Lord, of your deeds of salvation.**

In you, O Lord, I take refuge;
let me never be put to shame.
In your righteousness, deliver me and rescue me;
incline your ear to me and save me. R̰

Be to me a rock of refuge,
a strong fortress, to save me,
for you are my rock and my fortress.
Rescue me, O my God, from the hand of the wicked. R̰

For you, O Lord, are my hope,
my trust, O Lord, from my youth.
Upon you I have leaned from my birth;
from my mother's womb you have been my strength. R̰

My mouth will tell of your righteous acts,
of your deeds of salvation all day long.
O God, from my youth you have taught me,
and I still proclaim your wondrous deeds. R̰

The shorter version begins at the asterisks.

Brothers and sisters, strive for the greater gifts. And I will show you a still more excellent way.

If I speak in the tongues of human beings and of Angels, but do not have love, I am a noisy gong or a clanging cymbal. If I have prophetic powers, and understand all mysteries and all knowledge, and if I have all faith, so as to remove mountains, but do not have love, I am nothing. If I give away all my possessions, and if I hand over my body so that I may boast, but do not have love, I gain nothing.

* * *

Love is patient; love is kind; love is not envious or boastful or arrogant or rude. It does not insist on its own way; it is not irritable or resentful; it does not rejoice in wrongdoing, but rejoices in the truth. It bears all things, believes all things, hopes all things, endures all things. Love never ends.

But as for prophecies, they will come to an end; as for tongues, they will cease; as for knowledge, it will come to an end.

For we know only in part, and we prophesy only in part; but when the complete comes, the partial will come to an end.

When I was a child, I spoke like a child, I thought like a child, I reasoned like a child; when I became a man, I put an end to childish ways.

For now we see in a mirror, dimly, but then we will see face to face. Now I know only in part; then I will know fully, even as I have been fully known.

Now faith, hope, and love abide, these three; and the greatest of these is love.

The word of the Lord. **Thanks be to God.**

Jesus, filled with the power of the Spirit, came to Nazareth, where he had been brought up. He went to the synagogue on the Sabbath day, as was his custom, and read from the Prophet Isaiah. The eyes of all were fixed on him. Then he began to say to them, "Today this Scripture has been fulfilled in your hearing." All spoke well of him and were amazed at the gracious words that came from his mouth. They said, "Is not this Joseph's son?"

Jesus said to them, "Doubtless you will quote to me this proverb, 'Doctor, cure yourself!' And you will say, 'Do here also in your hometown the things that we have heard you did at Capernaum.'"

And he said, "Truly I tell you, no Prophet is accepted in his hometown. But the truth is, there were many widows in Israel in the time of Elijah, when the heaven was shut up three years and six months, and there was a severe famine over all the land; yet Elijah was sent to none of them except to a widow at Zarephath in Sidon. There were also many lepers in Israel in the time of the Prophet Elisha, and none of them was cleansed except Naaman the Syrian."

When they heard this, all in the synagogue were filled with rage. They got up, drove Jesus out of the town, and led him to the brow of the hill on which their town was built, so that they might hurl him off the cliff. But Jesus passed through the midst of them and went on his way.

The Gospel of the Lord. **Praise to you, Lord Jesus Christ.**

Do not break down is a phrase that is often heard in the Bible, spoken either by God or by a person God has sent to help the community. These words encourage us to be strong, stand firm and not to be afraid. As children of God we can live without fear for God is with us.

We live in hope because as Christians we know God will always help us. Many times in the Bible God promises to support and strengthen us, but the most certain sign of God's hope for us is that God sent us his Son, Jesus Christ.

When the complete comes is a phrase that refers to the moment in history when humanity will reach its fullness in God. Although nobody knows when this will occur, we have confidence that all women and men will finally live as sisters and brothers.

Isaiah was a friend of God who lived 700 years before Christ. He helped the people of Israel, especially those in Jerusalem, to avoid living in ways that offended God. His strong words moved people to change their ways and to have confidence in the forgiveness of God.

Elijah was a man who was very close to God. He lived 800 years before Christ. The Bible tells many extraordinary stories about Elijah's life, such as how he was carried to heaven in a chariot of fire.

Lepers are people who suffer from Hansen's disease or leprosy, a skin disease that once had no cure. Lepers were made to feel ashamed of how the disease ate away at their flesh and muscles. Healthy people were afraid because the disease is contagious, and felt that the sick person must have deserved to be ill because of their sins.

February 10

5th Sunday in Ordinary Time

A reading from the book of the Prophet Isaiah
(6.1-2, 3-8)

In the year that King Uzziah died, I saw the Lord sitting on a throne, high and lofty; and the hem of his robe filled the temple. Seraphs were in attendance above him; each had six wings. And one called to another and said: "Holy, holy, holy is the Lord of hosts; the whole earth is full of his glory." The pivots on the thresholds shook at the voices of those who called, and the house filled with smoke.

And I said: "Woe is me! I am lost, for I am a man of unclean lips, and I live among a people of unclean lips; yet my eyes have seen the King, the Lord of hosts!"

Then one of the seraphs flew to me, holding a live coal that had been taken from the altar with a pair of tongs. The seraph touched my mouth with it and said: "Now that this has touched your lips, your guilt has departed and your sin is blotted out."

Then I heard the voice of the Lord saying, "Whom shall I send, and who will go for us?" And I said, "Here am I; send me!"

The word of the Lord. **Thanks be to God.**

Psalm 138

R. **Before the Angels I sing your praise, O Lord.**

I give you thanks, O Lord, with my whole heart;
before the Angels I sing your praise;
I bow down toward your holy temple,
and give thanks to your name
for your steadfast love and your faithfulness. R.

For you have exalted your name
and your word above everything.
On the day I called, you answered me,
you increased my strength of soul. R.

All the kings of the earth shall praise you, O Lord,
for they have heard the words of your mouth.
They shall sing of the ways of the Lord,
for great is the glory of the Lord. R.

You stretch out your hand, and your right hand delivers me.
The Lord will fulfill his purpose for me;
your steadfast love, O Lord, endures forever.
Do not forsake the work of your hands. R.

A reading from the first Letter of Saint Paul to the Corinthians (15.1-11)

For the shorter version, omit the indented parts.

I would remind you,

Brothers and sisters,

of the good news that I proclaimed to you, which you in turn received, in which also you stand. This is the good news through which also you are being saved, if you hold firmly to the message that I proclaimed to you — unless you have come to believe in vain. For

I handed on to you as of first importance what I in turn had received: that Christ died for our sins in accordance with the Scriptures, and that he was buried, and that he was raised on the third day in accordance with the Scriptures, and that he appeared to Cephas, then to the twelve.

Then he appeared to more than five hundred of the brothers and sisters at one time, most of whom are still alive, though some have died. Then he appeared to James, then to all the Apostles. Last of all, as to one untimely born, he appeared also to me.

For I am the least of the Apostles, unfit to be called an Apostle, because I persecuted the Church of God. But by the grace of God I am what I am, and his grace toward me has not been in vain. On the contrary, I worked harder than any of the Apostles — though it was not I, but the grace of God that is with me.

Whether then it was I or they, so we proclaim and so you have come to believe.

The word of the Lord. **Thanks be to God.**

While Jesus was standing beside the lake of Gennesaret, and the crowd was pressing in on him to hear the word of God, he saw two boats there at the shore of the lake; the fishermen had gone out of them and were washing their nets.

Jesus got into one of the boats, the one belonging to Simon, and asked him to put out a little way from the shore. Then he sat down and taught the crowds from the boat. When he had finished speaking, he said to Simon, "Put out into the deep water and let down your nets for a catch." Simon answered, "Master, we have worked all night long but have caught nothing. Yet if you say so, I will let down the nets." When they had done this, they caught so many fish that their nets were beginning to break. So they signalled their partners in the other boat to come and help them. And they came and filled both boats, so that they began to sink.

But when Simon Peter saw it, he fell down at Jesus' knees, saying, "Go away from me, Lord, for I am a sinful man!"

For Simon Peter and all who were with him were amazed at the catch of fish that they had taken; and so also were James and John, sons of Zebedee, who were partners with Simon. Then Jesus said to Simon, "Do not be afraid; from now on you will be catching people."

When they had brought their boats to shore, they left everything and followed Jesus.

The Gospel of the Lord.
**Praise to you,
Lord Jesus Christ.**

King Uzziah was a king of Judah who reigned for over 50 years, 800 years before the birth of Christ . He brought peace and prosperity to his people, but he became very proud at the end of his life and was banished from the Temple.

When we use the word "glory" to refer to God, we are saying that we recognize God's power and importance, greatness and splendour.

A live coal is a piece of red-hot charcoal. When the angel "burned" Isaiah's lips with a live coal, it represented a cleansing from sin. Isaiah was so happy because he then knew that God had forgiven him his sins.

When Isaiah saw how his sins were forgiven and how great God's love was, he responded by saying, "Here am I; send me!" When we receive absolution in the Sacrament of Reconciliation, this should be our response, too.

Calling himself untimely born was Saint Paul's way of recognizing that, by the grace of God and not by his own merits, there had been a huge change in his life. He humbly accepted that this change was not due to his own efforts: his conversion was a special gift of grace from God.

The Lake of Gennesaret was also known as the Sea of Galilee or the Sea of Tiberias. It was the scene of many of Jesus' actions (such as preaching from a boat to the people on shore, the miracle of calming the stormy seas, and the miracle of the loaves and fish). Jesus was also seen there after his Resurrection.

When Jesus told Simon Peter, a fisherman, that he would now catch people, Jesus did not explain what this meant. But Simon Peter came to know that he was invited to dedicate his life so that others might know the Good News about the kingdom of God.

Ash Wednesday

Even now, says the Lord, return to me with all your heart, with fasting, with weeping, and with mourning; rend your hearts and not your clothing.

Return to the Lord, your God, for he is gracious and merciful, slow to anger, and abounding in steadfast love, and relents from punishing.

Who knows whether the Lord will not turn and relent, and leave a blessing behind him: a grain offering and a drink offering to be presented to the Lord, your God?

Blow the trumpet in Zion; sanctify a fast; call a solemn assembly; gather the people. Sanctify the congregation; assemble the aged; gather the children, even infants at the breast. Let the bridegroom leave his room, and the bride her canopy.

Between the vestibule and the altar let the priests, the ministers of the Lord, weep. Let them say, "Spare your people, O Lord, and do not make your heritage a mockery, a byword among the nations. Why should it be said among the peoples, 'Where is their God?'"

Then the Lord became jealous for his land, and had pity on his people.

The word of the Lord. **Thanks be to God.**

Psalm 51

R̫ **Have mercy, O Lord, for we have sinned.**

Have mercy on me, O God, according to your steadfast love;
according to your abundant mercy blot out my transgressions.
Wash me thoroughly from my iniquity,
and cleanse me from my sin. R̫

For I know my transgressions,
and my sin is ever before me.
Against you, you alone, have I sinned,
and done what is evil in your sight. R̫

Create in me a clean heart, O God,
and put a new and right spirit within me.
Do not cast me away from your presence,
and do not take your holy spirit from me. R̫

Restore to me the joy of your salvation,
and sustain in me a willing spirit.
O Lord, open my lips,
and my mouth will declare your praise. R̫

A reading from the second Letter of Saint Paul to the Corinthians (5.20 – 6.2)

Brothers and sisters: We are ambassadors for Christ, since God is making his appeal through us; we entreat you on behalf of Christ, be reconciled to God. For our sake God made Christ to be sin who knew no sin, so that in Christ we might become the righteousness of God. As we work together with him, we urge you also not to accept the grace of God in vain. For the Lord says, "At an acceptable time I have listened to you, and on a day of salvation I have helped you." See, now is the acceptable time; see, now is the day of salvation!

The word of the Lord. **Thanks be to God.**

A reading from the holy Gospel according to Matthew (6.1-6, 16-18)

Jesus said to the disciples: "Beware of practising your piety before people in order to be seen by them; for then you have no reward from your Father in heaven.

"So whenever you give alms, do not sound a trumpet before you, as the hypocrites do in the synagogues and in the streets, so that they may be praised by others. Truly I tell you, they have received their reward. But when you give alms, do not let your left hand know what your right hand is doing, so that your alms may be done in secret; and your Father who sees in secret will reward you.

"And whenever you pray, do not be like the hypocrites; for they love to stand and pray in the synagogues and at the street corners, so that they may be seen by others. Truly I tell you, they have received their reward. But whenever you pray, go into your room and shut the door and pray to your Father who is in secret; and your Father who sees in secret will reward you.

"And whenever you fast, do not look dismal, like the hypocrites, for they disfigure their faces so as to show others that they are fasting. Truly I tell you, they have received their reward. But when you fast, put oil on your head and wash your face, so that your fasting may be seen not by others but by your Father who is in secret; and your Father who sees in secret will reward you."

The Gospel of the Lord. **Praise to you, Lord Jesus Christ.**

Ash Wednesday marks the beginning of Lent. Ashes are used as a sign of our sorrow for having turned away from God; they are placed on our forehead in the sign of the cross and we wear them until they wear off. The ashes are often produced by burning palms from the previous year's Passion Sunday celebration.

To rend something is to tear it apart forcefully. In biblical times, people would tear their clothing and cover themselves with ashes as signs of their repentance. The Prophet Joel is saying that God would rather we rend or open our hearts as a sign of our willingness to return to God.

A congregation is a gathering of people, usually for worship. In the Hebrew Scriptures, it can also mean the whole people of God.

Ambassadors are messengers who have special authority to deliver a message or speak on someone else's behalf. Saint Paul is telling us that we have a special role to play as followers of Christ: we are chosen to spread the good news. If we are to be faithful messengers, then we must open our hearts and be reconciled to God.

To be reconciled means to be 'at-one' with someone, by making up for something wrong we may have done. Through his death, Jesus makes up for our sins and we are reconciled with God.

The three traditional Lenten practices are prayer, fasting and almsgiving. To give alms is to give money to the poor. The word comes from the Greek word for compassion or pity. During Lent, we not only focus on our own spiritual life, we also make a special effort to help those around us who are in need.

Hypocrites are people whose actions don't match their words. They may say they love God, but they don't act in a loving way. Such behaviour hurts that person, others around them and God.

1st Sunday of Lent

Moses spoke to the people, saying: "When the priest takes the basket from your hand and sets it down before the altar of the Lord your God, you shall make this response before the Lord your God:

"'A wandering Aramean was my father; he went down into Egypt and lived there as an alien, few in number, and there he became a great nation, mighty and populous. When the Egyptians treated us harshly and afflicted us, by imposing hard labour on us, we cried to the Lord, the God of our fathers; the Lord heard our voice and saw our affliction, our toil, and our oppression.

"'The Lord brought us out of Egypt with a mighty hand and an outstretched arm, with a terrifying display of power, and with signs and wonders; and he brought us into this place and gave us this land, a land flowing with milk and honey. So now I bring the first of the fruit of the ground that you, O Lord, have given me.'"

And Moses continued, "You shall set it down before the Lord your God and bow down before the Lord your God."

The word of the Lord. **Thanks be to God.**

Psalm 91

R. **Be with me, Lord, when I am in trouble.**

You who live in the shelter of the Most High,
who abide in the shadow of the Almighty,
will say to the Lord, "My refuge and my fortress;
my God, in whom I trust." R.

No evil shall befall you,
no scourge come near your tent.
For he will command his Angels concerning you
to guard you in all your ways. R.

On their hands they will bear you up,
so that you will not dash your foot against a stone.
You will tread on the lion and the adder,
the young lion and the serpent you will trample under foot. R.

The one who loves me, I will deliver;
I will protect the one who knows my name.
When he calls to me, I will answer him;
I will be with him in trouble, I will rescue him
and honour him. R.

A reading from the Letter of Saint Paul to the Romans (10.8-13)

Brothers and sisters, what does Scripture say?

"The word is near you, on your lips and in your heart" (that is, the word of faith that we proclaim); because if you confess with your lips that Jesus is Lord and believe in your heart that God raised him from the dead, you will be saved.

For one believes with the heart and so is justified, and one confesses with the mouth and so is saved.

The Scripture says, "No one who believes in him will be put to shame." For there is no distinction between Jew and Greek; the same Lord is Lord of all and is generous to all who call on him. For, "Everyone who calls on the name of the Lord shall be saved."

The word of the Lord. **Thanks be to God.**

A reading from the holy Gospel according to Luke (4.1-13)

Jesus, full of the Holy Spirit, returned from the Jordan and was led by the Spirit in the wilderness, where for forty days he was tempted by the devil. He ate nothing at all during those days, and when they were over, he was famished.

The devil said to him, "If you are the Son of God, command this stone to become a loaf of bread." Jesus answered him, "It is written, 'Man does not live by bread alone.'"

Then the devil led him up and showed him in an instant all the kingdoms of the world. And the devil said to him, "To you I will give their glory and all this authority; for it has been given over to me, and I give it to anyone I please. If you, then, will worship me, it will all be yours." Jesus answered him, "It is written, 'Worship the Lord your God, and serve only him.'"

Then the devil took him to Jerusalem, and placed him on the pinnacle of the temple, saying to him, "If you are the Son of God, throw yourself down from here, for it is written, 'He will command his Angels concerning you, to protect you,' and 'On their hands they will bear you up, so that you will not dash your foot against a stone.'" Jesus answered him, "It is said, 'Do not put the Lord your God to the test.'"

When the devil had finished every test, he departed from him until an opportune time.

The Gospel of the Lord. **Praise to you, Lord Jesus Christ.**

Deuteronomy is a book in the Old Testament or Hebrew Scriptures which teaches that there is only one God, and that the people of God should be united. Its name comes from the Greek word meaning "the second law" and refers to the second time that God gave the law to the people. It was written 600 years before Christ.

The altar is a table or rock upon which a sacrifice was offered to God: for example, an animal, some food or incense. Today, the altar is the table upon which the priest celebrates Mass, which is also a sacrifice — of Jesus Christ — that we offer to God.

The Arameans were a people that lived in Syria and Mesopotamia, parts of the Middle East. They were ancestors of the Hebrews.

To bow down is to bend deeply before someone, with your face on the ground, as a sign of respect, admiration and veneration. You would only do this before a person who was very important.

The Letter of Saint Paul to the Romans is the longest surviving letter that Saint Paul wrote. The Christians who lived in Rome belonged to a small community. Paul planned to travel to preach in Spain, and to stop on the way in Rome to visit the Christians. He sent this letter ahead in order to introduce himself, to encourage them, and to remind them of the teachings of Jesus.

The devil is the one who puts temptations before us so that we do not live as children of God. In today's Gospel, the devil tempts Jesus with worldly riches and power, hoping to turn Jesus away from God and his mission, but Jesus pays no attention to the devil.

February 24

2nd Sunday of Lent

The Lord said to Abram: "Look toward heaven and count the stars, if you are able to count them." Then he said to him, "So shall your descendants be." And he believed the Lord; and the Lord reckoned it to him as righteousness.

Then the Lord said to Abram, "I am the Lord who brought you from Ur of the Chaldeans, to give you this land to possess." But Abram said, "O Lord God, how am I to know that I shall possess it?"

The Lord said to him, "Bring me a heifer three years old, a female goat three years old, a ram three years old, a turtledove, and a young pigeon." Abram brought the Lord all these and cut them in two, laying each half over against the other; but he did not cut the birds in two. And when birds of prey came down on the carcasses, Abram drove them away.

As the sun was going down, a deep sleep fell upon Abram, and a deep and terrifying darkness descended upon him. When the sun had gone down and it was dark, a smoking fire pot and a flaming torch passed between these pieces.

On that day the Lord made a covenant with Abram, saying, "To your descendants I give this land, from the river of Egypt to the great river, the river Euphrates."

The word of the Lord. **Thanks be to God.**

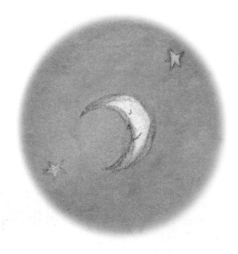

R⸝ **The Lord is my light and my salvation.**

The Lord is my light and my salvation;
whom shall I fear?
The Lord is the stronghold of my life;
of whom shall I be afraid? R⸝

Hear, O Lord, when I cry aloud,
be gracious to me and answer me!
"Come," my heart says, "seek his face!"
Your face, Lord, do I seek. R⸝

Do not hide your face from me.
Do not turn your servant away in anger,
you who have been my help.
Do not cast me off, do not forsake me,
     O God of my salvation! R⸝

I believe that I shall see the goodness of the Lord
in the land of the living.
Wait for the Lord; be strong,
and let your heart take courage; wait for the Lord! R⸝

A reading from the Letter of Saint Paul to the Philippians (3.17 – 4.1)

The shorter version begins at the asterisks.

Brothers and sisters, join in imitating me, and observe those who live according to the example you have in us. For many live as enemies of the Cross of Christ; I have often told you of them, and now I tell you even with tears. Their end is destruction; their god is the belly; and their glory is in their shame; their minds are set on earthly things.

* **

But our citizenship is in heaven, and it is from there that we are expecting a Saviour, the Lord Jesus Christ. He will transform the body of our humiliation that it may be conformed to the body of his glory, by the power that also enables him to make all things subject to himself.

Therefore, my brothers and sisters, whom I love and long for, my joy and crown, stand firm, my beloved, in the Lord in this way.

The word of the Lord. **Thanks be to God.**

Jesus took with him Peter and John and James, and went up on the mountain to pray. And while he was praying, the appearance of his face changed, and his clothes became dazzling white.

Suddenly they saw two men, Moses and Elijah, talking to Jesus. They appeared in glory and were speaking of his exodus, which he was about to accomplish at Jerusalem.

Now Peter and his companions were weighed down with sleep; but since they had stayed awake, they saw his glory and the two men who stood with him.

Just as they were leaving him, Peter said to Jesus, "Master, it is good for us to be here; let us make three dwellings, one for you, one for Moses, and one for Elijah," but Peter did not know what he said.

While he was saying this, a cloud came and overshadowed them; and they were terrified as they entered the cloud. Then from the cloud came a voice that said, "This is my Son, my Chosen; listen to him!" When the voice had spoken, Jesus was found alone.

And the disciples kept silent and in those days told no one any of the things they had seen.

The Gospel of the Lord.
**Praise to you,
Lord Jesus Christ.**

Genesis is the first book of the Bible. In it we find the stories of the creation of the world, the flood, the beginning of faith in God, and many other stories that show how the Hebrew people came to understand that God loved them and asked them to love God in return.

Abram is the first man who had true faith in God. God promised him that he'd have a prosperous life and many descendants, in return for being faithful and refusing to worship other gods. When Abram agreed, God gave him a new name, Abraham.

The Euphrates is an important river in Asia Minor that empties into the Persian Gulf. It flows through modern-day Turkey, Syria and Iraq. Together with the Tigris River, it irrigates what was once a very fertile area.

The Philippians were a community of Christians to whom Saint Paul wrote a friendly letter while he was in prison. Paul thanked them for sending money and encouraged them to continue to have faith in Jesus. Philippi is located in present-day northern Greece.

Peter, John and James were three apostles or friends of Jesus who accompanied him in the last years of his life. Jesus chose them to be near him during the most important moments, such as his Transfiguration, and to be witnesses of his Resurrection.

In this Gospel passage about the life of Jesus, a voice from a cloud said, "Listen to him." The three disciples then clearly understood that Jesus spoke with authority and that God wanted them to pay attention to all that Jesus taught them.

March 3

3rd Sunday of Lent

Moses was keeping the flock of his father-in-law Jethro, the priest of Midian; he led his flock beyond the wilderness, and came to Horeb, the mountain of God. There the Angel of the Lord appeared to him in a flame of fire out of a bush; Moses looked, and the bush was blazing, yet it was not consumed.

Then Moses said, "I must turn aside and look at this great sight, and see why the bush is not burned up."

When the Lord saw that Moses had turned aside to see, God called to him out of the bush, "Moses, Moses!" And Moses said, "Here I am." Then God said, "Come no closer! Remove the sandals from your feet, for the place on which you are standing is holy ground."

God said further, "I am the God of your fathers, the God of Abraham, the God of Isaac, and the God of Jacob." And Moses hid his face, for he was afraid to look at God.

Then the Lord said, "I have observed the misery of my people who are in Egypt; I have heard their cry on account of their taskmasters. Indeed, I know their sufferings, and I have come down to deliver them from the Egyptians, and to bring them up out of that land to a good and broad land, a land flowing with milk and honey."

But Moses said to God, "If I come to the children of Israel and say to them, 'The God of your fathers has sent me to you,' and they ask me, 'What is his name?' what shall I say to them?"

God said to Moses, "I AM WHO I AM" He said further, "Thus you shall say to the children of Israel, 'I AM has sent me to you.'"

God also said to Moses, "Thus you shall say to the children of Israel, 'The Lord, the God of your fathers, the God of Abraham, the God of Isaac, and the God of Jacob, has sent me to you.' This is my name forever, and this my memorial for all generations."

The word of the Lord. **Thanks be to God.**

R. **The Lord is merciful and gracious.**

Bless the Lord, O my soul,
and all that is within me, bless his holy name.
Bless the Lord, O my soul,
and do not forget all his benefits. R.

It is the Lord who forgives all your iniquity,
who heals all your diseases,
who redeems your life from the Pit,
who crowns you with steadfast love and mercy. R.

The Lord works vindication
and justice for all who are oppressed.
He made known his ways to Moses,
his acts to the people of Israel. R.

The Lord is merciful and gracious,
slow to anger and abounding in steadfast love.
For as the heavens are high above the earth,
so great is his steadfast love toward those who fear him. R.

A reading from the first Letter of Saint Paul to the Corinthians (10.1-6, 10-12)

I do not want you to be unaware, brothers and sisters, that our ancestors were all under the cloud; all passed through the sea; all were baptized into Moses in the cloud and in the sea; all ate the same spiritual food, and all drank the same spiritual drink. For they drank from the spiritual rock that followed them, and the rock was Christ.

Nevertheless, God was not pleased with most of them, and they were struck down in the wilderness.

Now these things occurred as examples for us, so that we might not desire evil as they did. And do not complain as some of them did, and were destroyed by the destroyer.

These things happened to them to serve as an example, and they were written down to instruct us, on whom the ends of the ages have come. So if you think you are standing, watch out that you do not fall.

The word of the Lord. **Thanks be to God.**

Jesus was teaching the crowds; some of those present told Jesus about the Galileans whose blood Pilate had mingled with their sacrifices.

Jesus asked them, "Do you think that because these Galileans suffered in this way they were worse sinners than all other Galileans? No, I tell you; but unless you repent, you will all perish as they did. Or those eighteen who were killed when the tower of Siloam fell on them — do you think that they were worse offenders than all the others living in Jerusalem? No, I tell you; but unless you repent, you will all perish just as they did."

Then Jesus told this parable: "A man had a fig tree planted in his vineyard; and he came looking for fruit on it and found none. So he said to the gardener, 'See here! For three years I have come looking for fruit on this fig tree, and still I find none. Cut it down! Why should it be wasting the soil?'

"The gardener replied, 'Sir, let it alone for one more year, until I dig around it and put manure on it. If it bears fruit next year, well and good; but if not, you can cut it down.'"

The Gospel of the Lord.
**Praise to you,
Lord Jesus Christ.**

111

The second book of the Bible is called Exodus. It is an important book because it tells how God liberated his people from slavery in Egypt, made a covenant with them and gave them the Ten Commandments, which taught them how to live correctly. In addition to these stories, the book of Exodus outlines laws and explains how to prepare certain celebrations, such as the Passover.

The Hebrew God was known by four letters: YHWH. This name means, "I am who I am," taken from the verb "to be." This name shows that God is the origin of all being and the giver of life.

Saul was a Jew who persecuted the Christians, but thanks to an encounter with the risen Christ, he stopped persecuting Christians and became a follower of Jesus. His change was so radical that he even changed his name to Paul. Paul was a great Christian apostle. He travelled far and wide to preach the Gospel. He wrote many important letters that came to form a large part of the New Testament or Christian Scriptures.

The ancestors Saint Paul refers to were those who left slavery in Egypt and who wandered in the desert for forty years before coming to the Promised Land. Because they lived before the time of Christ, they did not know Jesus, but God was faithful to the covenant he had made with them.

Although God had released his people from slavery in Egypt, they grew discontented and desired to return to their old way of life. Saint Paul warns us not to make the same mistake, but to desire a life of faithfulness to God and his promises.

Pontius Pilate was the Roman governor of Judea, the southern part of Israel. This is the same Pilate who condemned Jesus to die on the cross.

March 10

4th Sunday of Lent

A reading from the book of Joshua (5.9, 10-12)

The Lord said to Joshua, "Today I have rolled away from you the disgrace of Egypt."

While the children of Israel were camped in Gilgal they kept the Passover in the evening on the fourteenth day of the month in the plains of Jericho.

On the day after the Passover, on that very day, they ate the produce of the land, unleavened cakes and parched grain. The manna ceased on the day they ate the produce of the land, and the children of Israel no longer had manna; they ate the crops of the land of Canaan that year.

The word of the Lord. **Thanks be to God.**

Psalm 34

R. **Taste and see that the Lord is good.**

I will bless the Lord at all times;
his praise shall continually be in my mouth.
My soul makes its boast in the Lord;
let the humble hear and be glad. R.

O magnify the Lord with me,
and let us exalt his name together.
I sought the Lord, and he answered me,
and delivered me from all my fears. R.

Look to him, and be radiant;
so your faces shall never be ashamed.
The poor one called, and the Lord heard,
and saved that person from every trouble. R.

Brothers and sisters: If anyone is in Christ, there is a new creation: everything old has passed away; see, everything has become new! All this is from God, who reconciled us to himself through Christ, and has given us the ministry of reconciliation; that is, in Christ, God was reconciling the world to himself, not counting their trespasses against them, and entrusting the message of reconciliation to us.

So we are ambassadors for Christ, since God is making his appeal through us; we entreat you on behalf of Christ, be reconciled to God. For our sake God made Christ to be sin who knew no sin, so that in Christ we might become the righteousness of God.

The word of the Lord. **Thanks be to God.**

All the tax collectors and sinners were coming near to listen to Jesus. And the Pharisees and the scribes were grumbling and saying, "This fellow welcomes sinners and eats with them."

So he told them a parable: "There was a man who had two sons. The younger of them said to his father, 'Father, give me the share of the property that will belong to me.' So the father divided his property between them. A few days later the younger son gathered all he had and travelled to a distant country, and there he squandered his property in dissolute living.

"When he had spent everything, a severe famine took place throughout that country, and he began to be in need. So he went and hired himself out to one of the citizens of that country, who sent him to his fields to feed the pigs. The young man would gladly have filled himself with the pods that the pigs were eating; and no one gave him anything.

"But when he came to himself he said, 'How many of my father's hired hands have bread enough and to spare, but here I am dying of hunger! I will get up and go to my father, and I will say to him, "Father, I have sinned against heaven and before you; I am no longer worthy to be called your son; treat me like one of your hired hands."'

"So he set off and went to his father. But while he was still far off, his father saw him and was filled with compassion; he ran and put his arms around him and kissed him.

"Then the son said to him, 'Father, I have sinned against heaven and before you; I am no longer worthy to be called your son.' But the father said to his slaves, 'Quickly, bring out a robe — the best one — and put it on him; put a ring on his finger and sandals on his feet. And get the fatted calf and kill it, and let us eat and celebrate; for this son of mine was dead and is alive again; he was lost and is found!' And they began to celebrate.

"Now his elder son was in the field; and when he came and approached the house, he heard music and dancing. He called one of the slaves and asked what was going on. The slave replied, 'Your brother has come, and your father has killed the fatted calf, because he has got him back safe and sound.'

"Then the elder son became angry and refused to go in. His father came out and began to plead with him. But he answered his father, 'Listen! For all these years I have been working like a slave for you, and I have never disobeyed your command; yet you have never given me even a young goat so that I might celebrate with my friends. But when this son of yours came back, who has devoured your property with prostitutes, you killed the fatted calf for him!'

"Then the father said to him, 'Son, you are always with me, and all that is mine is yours. But we had to celebrate and rejoice, because this brother of yours was dead and has come to life; he was lost and has been found.'"

The Gospel of the Lord. **Praise to you, Lord Jesus Christ.**

When Moses died, God gave Joshua the responsibility of taking the people of Israel to conquer the Promised Land. The book of Joshua in the Bible tells of this conquest and how the land was divided among the twelve tribes of Israel.

The Jewish festival to celebrate the liberation of the Hebrew people is called Passover. They recall how the angel of the Lord came to convince Pharaoh to let the slaves go free. They remember their passage through the Red Sea. For Christians, Easter is the most important feast day, as we remember Jesus' resurrection: how he passed from death to life.

Unleavened cakes are made from wheat flour without the addition of yeast or leaven. This bread does not rise, resembling a crepe or pita. Jesus used unleavened bread at the Last Supper, because he and his disciples were having their Passover meal.

Manna is the food that God let fall upon the Israelites when they were crossing the desert and had nothing to eat. Manna was called "bread from heaven."

When we read that it was God who reconciled us to himself, we understand that God forgave us and took away all the reasons he had to be angry or upset with us. God also gave to the apostles the mission to reconcile everything to God and to reconcile human beings to each another. This is a vocation for all the Church.

The tax collectors were local men who worked for the Romans, and therefore were seen as traitors and despised by the Jews. Many tax collectors were also cheats, taking more money than was their due.

March 17

5th Sunday of Lent

Thus says the Lord,
who makes a way in the sea,
a path in the mighty waters,
who brings out chariot and horse, army and warrior;
they lie down, they cannot rise,
they are extinguished, quenched like a wick:
"Do not remember the former things,
or consider the things of old.

"I am about to do a new thing;
now it springs forth, do you not perceive it?
I will make a way in the wilderness
and rivers in the desert.

"The wild animals will honour me,
the jackals and the ostriches;
for I give water in the wilderness, rivers in the desert,
to give drink to my chosen people,
the people whom I formed for myself
so that they might declare my praise."

The word of the Lord. **Thanks be to God.**

Psalm 126

R̩ **The Lord has done great things for us;
we are filled with joy.**

When the Lord restored the fortunes of Zion,
we were like those who dream.
Then our mouth was filled with laughter,
and our tongue with shouts of joy. R̩

Then it was said among the nations,
"The Lord has done great things for them."
The Lord has done great things for us,
and we rejoiced. R̩ →

R. **The Lord has done great things for us;**
we are filled with joy.

Restore our fortunes, O Lord,
like the watercourses in the desert of the Negev.
May those who sow in tears
reap with shouts of joy. R.

Those who go out weeping,
bearing the seed for sowing,
shall come home with shouts of joy,
carrying their sheaves. R.

A reading from the Letter of Saint Paul to the Philippians   (3.8-14)

Brothers and sisters: I regard everything as loss because of the surpassing value of knowing Christ Jesus my Lord. For his sake I have suffered the loss of all things, and I regard them as rubbish, in order that I may gain Christ and be found in him, not having a righteousness of my own that comes from the law, but one that comes through faith in Christ, the righteousness from God based on faith.

I want to know Christ and the power of his resurrection and the sharing of his sufferings by becoming like him in his death, if somehow I may attain the resurrection from the dead.

Not that I have already obtained this or have already reached the goal; but I press on to make it my own, because Christ Jesus has made me his own.

Brothers and sisters, I do not consider that I have made it my own; but this one thing I do: forgetting what lies behind and straining forward to what lies ahead, I press on toward the goal for the prize of the heavenly call of God in Christ Jesus.

The word of the Lord. **Thanks be to God.**

Jesus went to the Mount of Olives. Early in the morning he came again to the temple. All the people came to him and he sat down and began to teach them.

The scribes and the Pharisees brought a woman who had been caught in adultery; and making her stand before the people, they said to Jesus, "Teacher, this woman was caught in the very act of committing adultery. In the law, Moses commanded us to stone such women. Now what do you say?" They said this to test Jesus, so that they might have some charge to bring against him.

Jesus bent down and wrote with his finger on the ground. When the scribes and Pharisees kept on questioning him, Jesus straightened up and said to them, "Let anyone among you who is without sin be the first to throw a stone at her." And once again Jesus bent down and wrote on the ground.

When the scribes and Pharisees heard what Jesus had said, they went away, one by one, beginning with the elders; and Jesus was left alone with the woman standing before him.

Jesus straightened up and said to her, "Woman, where are they? Has no one condemned you?" She said, "No one, sir." And Jesus said, "Neither do I condemn you. Go your way, and from now on do not sin again."

The Gospel of the Lord.
Praise to you, Lord Jesus Christ.

121

Isaiah was a Prophet who lived 800 years before Christ. His role was to help the people of Israel, especially in Jerusalem, to understand that their way of life offended God. His words moved the people to change and to have confidence in God's pardon.

The words "makes a way in the sea" remind us of the Israelites' crossing of the Red Sea, when God opened the waters so that the people could escape Pharaoh's army and slavery in Egypt.

Saint John is the author of the fourth gospel, as well as the book of Revelation and three letters of the New Testament. John was one of the twelve apostles and Jesus loved him dearly. He accompanied Jesus in important moments, such as the Transfiguration, and he stood at the foot of the cross with Jesus' mother Mary.

Adultery refers to a deep breakdown in trust between spouses. To be caught in the very act of adultery means to be discovered in the very moment when a sin is being committed.

When Jesus says to the woman, "Go your way, and from now on do not sin again," the pardon that he offers is complete. Jesus tells her to resume her life as a new person, freed from the burden of her misdeeds.

March 24

Passion Sunday

A reading from the holy Gospel according to Luke
(19.28-40)

Jesus went on ahead, going up to Jerusalem. When he had come near Bethphage and Bethany, at the place called the Mount of Olives, he sent two of the disciples, saying, "Go into the village ahead of you, and as you enter it you will find tied there a colt that has never been ridden. Untie it and bring it here. If anyone asks you, 'Why are you untying it?' just say this, 'The Lord needs it.'"

So those who were sent departed and found it as Jesus had told them. As they were untying the colt, its owners asked them, "Why are you untying the colt?" They said, "The Lord needs it."

Then they brought the colt to Jesus; and after throwing their cloaks on the colt, they set Jesus on it.

As he rode along, people kept spreading their cloaks on the road. As he was now approaching the path down from the Mount of Olives, the whole multitude of the disciples began to praise God joyfully, and with a loud voice, for all the deeds of power that they had seen, saying, "Blessed is the king who comes in the name of the Lord! Peace in heaven, and glory in the highest heaven!"

Some of the Pharisees in the crowd said to him, "Teacher, order your disciples to stop."

Jesus answered, "I tell you, if these were silent, the stones would shout out."

The Gospel of the Lord. **Praise to you, Lord Jesus Christ.**

A reading from the book of the Prophet Isaiah (50.4-7)

The servant of the Lord said: "The Lord God has given me the tongue of a teacher, that I may know how to sustain the weary with a word. Morning by morning he wakens — wakens my ear to listen as those who are taught.

"The Lord God has opened my ear, and I was not rebellious, I did not turn backward.

"I gave my back to those who struck me, and my cheeks to those who pulled out the beard; I did not hide my face from insult and spitting.

"The Lord God helps me; therefore I have not been disgraced; therefore I have set my face like flint, and I know that I shall not be put to shame."

The word of the Lord. **Thanks be to God.**

124

R. **My God, my God, why have you forsaken me?**

All who see me mock at me;
they make mouths at me, they shake their heads;
"Commit your cause to the Lord; let him deliver;
let him rescue the one in whom he delights!" R.

For dogs are all around me;
a company of evildoers encircles me.
My hands and feet have shrivelled;
I can count all my bones. R.

They divide my clothes among themselves,
and for my clothing they cast lots.
But you, O Lord, do not be far away!
O my help, come quickly to my aid! R.

I will tell of your name to my brothers and sisters;
in the midst of the congregation I will praise you:
You who fear the Lord, praise him!
All you offspring of Jacob, glorify him;
stand in awe of him, all you offspring of Israel! R.

A reading from the Letter of Saint Paul to the Philippians (2.6-11)

Christ Jesus, though he was in the form of God, did not regard equality with God as something to be exploited, but emptied himself, taking the form of a slave, being born in human likeness. And being found in human form, he humbled himself and became obedient to the point of death — even death on a cross.

Therefore God highly exalted him and gave him the name that is above every name, so that at the name of Jesus every knee should bend, in heaven and on earth and under the earth, and every tongue should confess that Jesus Christ is Lord, to the glory of God the Father.

The word of the Lord. **Thanks be to God.**

A reading from the holy Gospel according to Luke
(22.14 – 23.56)

Several readers may proclaim the passion narrative today. N indicates the narrator, J the words of Jesus, and S the words of other speakers.

N   The Passion of our Lord Jesus Christ according to Luke.

When the hour came, Jesus took his place at the table, and the Apostles with him. He said to them,

J   **I have eagerly desired to eat this Passover with you before I suffer; for I tell you, I will not eat it until it is fulfilled in the kingdom of God.**

N   Then he took a cup, and after giving thanks he said,

J   **Take this and divide it among yourselves; for I tell you that from now on I will not drink of the fruit of the vine until the kingdom of God comes.**

N   Then Jesus took a loaf of bread, and when he had given thanks, he broke it and gave it to them, saying,

J   **This is my Body, which is given for you. Do this in remembrance of me.**

N   And he did the same with the cup after supper, saying,

J   **This cup that is poured out for you is the new covenant in my Blood. But see, the one who betrays me is with me, and his hand is on the table. For the Son of Man is going as it has been determined, but woe to that one by whom he is betrayed!**

N   Then they began to ask one another, which one of them it could be who would do this. A dispute also arose among them as to which one of them was to be regarded as the greatest. But Jesus said to them,

J   **The kings of the Gentiles lord it over them; and those in authority over them are called benefactors.**

But not so with you; rather the greatest among you must become like the youngest, and the leader like one who serves. For who is greater, the one who is at the table or the one who serves? Is it not the one at the table? But I am among you as one who serves.

You are those who have stood by me in my trials; and I confer on you, just as my Father has conferred on me, a kingdom, so that you may eat and drink at my table in my kingdom, and you will sit on thrones judging the twelve tribes of Israel.

Simon, Simon, listen! Satan has demanded to sift all of you like wheat, but I have prayed for you that your own faith may not fail; and you, when once you have turned back, strengthen your brothers.

N And Peter said to Jesus,

S *Lord, I am ready to go with you to prison and to death!*

J I tell you, Peter, the cock will not crow this day, until you have denied three times that you know me.

N Then Jesus said to the Apostles,

J When I sent you out without a purse, bag, or sandals, did you lack anything?

S *No, not a thing.*

J But now, the one who has a purse must take it, and likewise a bag. And the one who has no sword must sell his cloak and buy one. For I tell you, this Scripture must be fulfilled in me, "And he was counted among the lawless"; and indeed what is written about me is being fulfilled.

S *Lord, look, here are two swords.*

J It is enough.

N Jesus came out and went, as was his custom, to the Mount of Olives; and the disciples followed him. When he reached the place, he said to his disciples,

J Pray that you may not come into the time of temptation.

N Then Jesus withdrew from them about a stone's throw, knelt down, and prayed,

J Father, if you are willing, remove this cup from me; yet, not my will but yours be done.

N Then an Angel from heaven appeared to Jesus and gave him strength. In his anguish he prayed more earnestly, and his sweat became like great drops of blood falling down on the ground.

When Jesus got up from prayer, he came to the disciples and found them sleeping because of grief, and he said to them,

J   **Why are you sleeping? Get up and pray that you may not come into the time of temptation.**

N   While Jesus was still speaking, suddenly a crowd came, and the one called Judas, one of the twelve, was leading them. He approached Jesus to kiss him; but Jesus said to him,

J   **Judas, is it with a kiss that you are betraying the Son of Man?**

N   When those who were around Jesus saw what was coming, they asked,

S   *Lord, should we strike with the sword?*

N   Then one of the disciples struck the slave of the high priest and cut off his right ear. But Jesus said,

J   **No more of this!**

N   And Jesus touched the slave's ear and healed him. Then Jesus said to the chief priests, the officers of the temple police, and the elders who had come for him,

J   **Have you come out with swords and clubs as if I were a bandit? When I was with you day after day in the temple, you did not lay hands on me. But this is your hour, and the** power of darkness!

N   Then they seized Jesus and led him away, bringing him into the high priest's house. But Peter was following at a distance. When they had kindled a fire in the middle of the courtyard and sat down together, Peter sat among them. Then a servant girl, seeing him in the firelight, stared at him and said,

S   *This man also was with him.*

N   But Peter denied it, saying,

S   *Woman, I do not know him.*

N   A little later someone else, on seeing him, said,

S   *You also are one of them.*

N   But Peter said,

S   *Man, I am not!*

N   Then about an hour later still another kept insisting,

S   *Surely this man also was with him; for he is a Galilean.*

N   But Peter said,

S   *Man, I do not know what you are talking about!*

N At that moment, while he was still speaking, the cock crowed. The Lord turned and looked at Peter. Then Peter remembered the word of the Lord, how he had said to him, "Before the cock crows today, you will deny me three times." And Peter went out and wept bitterly.

Now the men who were holding Jesus began to mock him and beat him; they also blindfolded him and kept asking him,

S *Prophesy! Who is it that struck you?*

N They kept heaping many other insults on him.

When day came, the assembly of the elders of the people, both chief priests and scribes, gathered together, and they brought Jesus to their council. They said,

S *If you are the Christ, tell us.*

J If I tell you, you will not believe; and if I question you, you will not answer. But from now on the Son of Man will be seated at the right hand of the power of God.

N All of them asked,

S *Are you, then, the Son of God?*

J You say that I am.

S *What further testimony do we need? We have heard it ourselves from his own lips!*

N Then the assembly rose as a body and brought Jesus before Pilate. They began to accuse him, saying,

S *We found this man perverting our nation, forbidding us to pay taxes to the emperor, and saying that he himself is the Christ, a king.*

N Then Pilate asked Jesus,

S *Are you the king of the Jews?*

J You say so.

N Then Pilate said to the chief priests and the crowds,

S *I find no basis for an accusation against this man.*

N But they were insistent and said,

S *He stirs up the people by teaching throughout all Judea, from Galilee where he began even to this place.*

N When Pilate heard this, he asked whether the man was a Galilean. And when he learned that he was under Herod's jurisdiction, he sent him off to Herod, who was himself in Jerusalem at that time.

When Herod saw Jesus, he was very glad, for he had been wanting to see him for a long time, because he had heard about him and was hoping to see Jesus perform some sign.

Herod questioned him at some length, but Jesus gave him no answer. The chief priests and the scribes stood by, vehemently accusing him.

Even Herod with his soldiers treated him with contempt and mocked him; then he put an elegant robe on him, and sent him back to Pilate. That same day Herod and Pilate became friends with each other; before this they had been enemies.

Pilate then called together the chief priests, the leaders, and the people, and said to them,

S *You brought me this man as one who was perverting the people; and here I have examined him in your presence and have not found this man guilty of any of your charges against him. Neither has Herod, for he sent him back to us. Indeed, he has done nothing to deserve death. I will therefore have him flogged and release him.*

N Now Pilate was obliged to release someone for them at the festival. Then they all shouted out together,

S *Away with this fellow! Release Barabbas for us.*

N This was a man who had been put in prison for an insurrection that had taken place in the city, and for murder.

Pilate, wanting to release Jesus, addressed them again; but they kept shouting,

S *Crucify, crucify him!*

N A third time Pilate said to them,

S *Why, what evil has he done? I have found in him no ground for the sentence of death; I will therefore have him flogged and then release him.*

N But they kept urgently demanding with loud shouts that he should be crucified; and their voices prevailed. So Pilate gave his verdict that their demand should be granted. He released the man they asked for, the one who had been put in prison for insurrection and murder, and he handed Jesus over as they wished.

As they led Jesus away, they seized a man, Simon of Cyrene, who was coming from the country, and they laid the Cross on him, and made him carry it behind Jesus.

A great number of the people followed him, and among them were women who were beating their breasts and wailing for him. But Jesus turned to them and said,

J   Daughters of Jerusalem, do not weep for me, but weep for yourselves and for your children. For the days are surely coming when they will say, "Blessed are the barren, and the wombs that never bore, and the breasts that never nursed." Then they will begin to say to the mountains, "Fall on us," and to the hills, "Cover us." For if they do this when the wood is green, what will happen when it is dry?

N   Two others also, who were criminals, were led away to be put to death with Jesus. When they came to the place that is called The Skull, they crucified Jesus there with the criminals, one on his right and one on his left. Then Jesus said,

J   Father, forgive them; for they do not know what they are doing.

N   And they cast lots to divide his clothing. And the people stood by, watching; but the leaders scoffed at him, saying,

S   *He saved others; let him save himself if he is the Christ of God, his chosen one!*

N   The soldiers also mocked Jesus, coming up and offering him sour wine, and saying,

S   *If you are the King of the Jews, save yourself!*

N   There was also an inscription over him, "This is the King of the Jews."

One of the criminals who were hanged there kept deriding him and saying,

S   *Are you not the Christ? Save yourself and us!*

N   But the other criminal rebuked the first, saying,

S   *Do you not fear God, since you are under the same sentence of condemnation? And we indeed have been condemned justly, for we are getting what we deserve for our deeds, but this man has done nothing wrong.*

N   Then he said,

S   *Jesus, remember me when you come into your kingdom.*

J   **Truly I tell you, today you will be with me in Paradise.**

N   It was now about noon, and darkness came over the whole land until three in the afternoon, while the sun's light failed; and the curtain of the temple was torn in two. Then Jesus, crying with a loud voice, said,

J   **Father, into your hands I commend my spirit.**

N   Having said this, he breathed his last.

Here all kneel and pause for a short time.

N   When the centurion saw what had taken place, he praised God and said,

S   *Certainly this man was innocent.*

N   And when all the crowds who had gathered there for this spectacle saw what had taken place, they returned home, beating their breasts.

But all his acquaintances, including the women who had followed him from Galilee, stood at a distance, watching these things.

Now there was a good and righteous man named Joseph, who, though a member of the council, had not agreed to their plan and action. He came from the Jewish town of Arimathea, and he was waiting expectantly for the kingdom of God. This man went to Pilate and asked for the body of Jesus. Then he took it down, wrapped it in a linen cloth, and laid it in a rock-hewn tomb where no one had ever been laid.

It was the day of Preparation, and the Sabbath was beginning. The women who had come with Jesus from Galilee followed, and they saw the tomb and how his body was laid. Then they returned, and prepared spices and ointments. On the Sabbath these women rested according to the commandment.

An important task of a prophet (and also of the Church and all Christians) is to sustain the weary — to give strength to those who have fallen or who are weak, to offer hope to the hopeless and comfort to the lonely, and to bring consolation to those who mourn.

To be exploited is to be taken advantage of by someone who hopes to gain from our loss. Exploitation is a tyranny of the powerful over the weak.

When we read that Christ emptied himself, it means that he set aside his exalted or glorious condition as God in order to become a human person like us. Jesus' sacrifice was total: he gave all he was and had for our salvation.

When we come before Jesus, we realize we are in the presence of someone great and awe-inspiring. We bow down before Jesus, because every knee should bend before God.

All of us will live in the kingdom of God. This will happen when all of humanity allows God's love to move us. We are called to live as children of God and love one another as sisters and brothers.

At times when it seems like evil or sin has taken over our lives or our world, it may seem that the power of darkness is strong. When Jesus died, his friends felt this way. However, Jesus' resurrection is proof that darkness and death have no final control over us, because Jesus conquered death.

The Romans controlled the land where Jesus lived and the people were forced to pay taxes to the emperor. Although Jesus never opposed these payments, he was falsely accused of this when he was taken before the governor, Pilate.

March 31

The Resurrection of the Lord
Easter Sunday

Peter began to speak: "You know the message that spread throughout Judea, beginning in Galilee after the baptism that John announced: how God anointed Jesus of Nazareth with the Holy Spirit and with power; how he went about doing good and healing all who were oppressed by the devil, for God was with him.

"We are witnesses to all that he did both in Judea and in Jerusalem. They put him to death by hanging him on a tree; but God raised him on the third day and allowed him to appear, not to all the people but to us who were chosen by God as witnesses, and who ate and drank with him after he rose from the dead.

"He commanded us to preach to the people and to testify that he is the one ordained by God as judge of the living and the dead. All the Prophets testify about him that everyone who believes in him receives forgiveness of sins through his name."

The word of the Lord. **Thanks be to God.**

Psalm 118

R̰ **This is the day the Lord has made;
let us rejoice and be glad.**

or **Alleluia! Alleluia! Alleluia!**

O give thanks to the Lord, for he is good;
his steadfast love endures forever.
Let Israel say,
"His steadfast love endures forever." R̰

"The right hand of the Lord is exalted;
the right hand of the Lord does valiantly."
I shall not die, but I shall live,
and recount the deeds of the Lord. R̰

The stone that the builders rejected
has become the chief cornerstone.
This is the Lord's doing;
it is marvellous in our eyes. R̰

An alternate reading follows.

A reading from the Letter of Saint Paul to the Colossians (3.1-4)

Brothers and sisters: If you have been raised with Christ, seek the things that are above, where Christ is, seated at the right hand of God. Set your minds on things that are above, not on things that are on earth, for you have died, and your life is hidden with Christ in God. When Christ who is your life is revealed, then you also will be revealed with him in glory.

The word of the Lord. **Thanks be to God.**

or

A reading from the first Letter of Saint Paul to the Corinthians (5.6-8)

Do you not know that a little yeast leavens the whole batch of dough? Clean out the old yeast so that you may be a new batch, as you really are unleavened. For our paschal lamb, Christ, has been sacrificed. Therefore, let us celebrate the festival, not with the old yeast, the yeast of malice and evil, but with the unleavened bread of sincerity and truth.

The word of the Lord. **Thanks be to God.**

A reading from the holy Gospel according to John (20.1-18)

The shorter version ends at the asterisks.

Early on the first day of the week, while it was still dark, Mary Magdalene came to the tomb and saw that the stone had been removed from the tomb. So she ran and went to Simon Peter and the other disciple, the one whom Jesus loved, and said to them, "They have taken the Lord out of the tomb, and we do not know where they have laid him."

Then Peter and the other disciple set out and went toward the tomb. The two were running together, but the other disciple outran Peter and reached the tomb first. He bent down to look in and saw the linen wrappings lying there, but he did not go in.

Then Simon Peter came, following him, and went into the tomb. He saw the linen wrappings lying there, and the cloth that had been on Jesus' head, not lying with the linen wrappings but rolled up in a place by itself. Then the other disciple, who reached the tomb first, also went in, and he saw and believed; for as yet they did not understand the Scripture, that he must rise from the dead.

***

Then the disciples returned to their homes. But Mary Magdalene stood weeping outside the tomb. As she wept, she bent over to look into the tomb; and she saw two Angels in white, sitting where the body of Jesus had been lying, one at the head and the other at the feet. They said to her, "Woman, why are you weeping?" She said to them, "They have taken away my Lord, and I do not know where they have laid him."

When she had said this, she turned around and saw Jesus standing there, but she did not know that it was Jesus. Jesus said to her, "Woman, why are you weeping? Whom are you looking for?" Supposing him to be the gardener, she said to him, "Sir, if you have carried him away, tell me where you have laid him, and I will take him away."

Jesus said to her, "Mary!" She turned and said to him in Hebrew, "Rabbouni!" which means Teacher. Jesus said to her, "Do not hold on to me, because I have not yet ascended to the Father. But go to my brothers and say to them, 'I am ascending to my Father and your Father, to my God and your God.'"

Mary Magdalene went and announced to the disciples, "I have seen the Lord," and she told them that he had said these things to her.

The Gospel of the Lord.
Praise to you, Lord Jesus Christ.

The Acts of the Apostles is a book in the New Testament or Christian Scriptures that describes how the Church grew after Jesus rose from the dead. It was written by Saint Luke, who also wrote a Gospel.

To anoint means to "bless with oil." In the Bible it can also mean to give someone a mission, an important job. God anoints Jesus with the Holy Spirit to show that God was giving Jesus his mission. Christians are anointed at baptism and confirmation: our mission is to live as Jesus taught us.

God raised him: Jesus' resurrection, his passing through death to eternal life, is the most important element of the Christian faith. We believe that Jesus did not remain dead in the tomb, but overcame death, suffering and sin. We want to live as he taught, in order to be united with him now and in the next life.

The Prophets were good men and women who spoke for God. Sometimes their message was harsh: they asked people to make big changes in their lives and attitudes in order to grow closer to God. At other times, they brought words of comfort.

Saint Paul wrote to the Colossians, a Christian community at Colossae in modern-day Turkey, to help them to understand that Jesus Christ is above everything. No powers are greater than he is.

The things that are above, that is, in heaven, are those that Jesus teaches: finding the truth, living simply, trusting in God, and caring for those in need. The things of earth distract us from Jesus: being selfish, hurting others and ignoring the poor.

The linen wrappings were the fabric that covered the body of a dead person in the tomb. Joseph of Arimathea and Nicodemus made sure that Jesus' body was treated with dignity and buried properly: they covered his face and then wrapped his body with linen wrappings.

2nd Sunday of Easter

A reading from the Acts of the Apostles (5.12-16)

Many signs and wonders were done among the people through the Apostles. And the believers were all together in Solomon's Portico. None of the rest dared to join them, but the people held them in high esteem.

Yet more than ever believers were added to the Lord, great numbers of both men and women, so that they even carried out the sick into the streets, and laid them on cots and mats, in order that Peter's shadow might fall on some of them as he came by.

A great number of people would also gather from the towns around Jerusalem, bringing the sick and those tormented by unclean spirits, and they were all cured.

The word of the Lord. **Thanks be to God.**

Psalm 118

R̰ **Give thanks to the Lord, for he is good;
his steadfast love endures forever.**

or **Alleluia!**

Let Israel say,
"His steadfast love endures forever."
Let the house of Aaron say,
"His steadfast love endures forever."
Let those who fear the Lord say,
"His steadfast love endures forever." R̰

The stone that the builders rejected
has become the chief cornerstone.
This is the Lord's doing;
it is marvellous in our eyes.
This is the day that the Lord has made;
let us rejoice and be glad in it. R̰

Save us, we beseech you, O Lord!
O Lord, we beseech you, give us success!
Blessed is the one who comes in the name of the Lord.
We bless you from the house of the Lord.
The Lord is God,
and he has given us light. R̰

A reading from the book of Revelation
(1.9-11, 12-13, 17-19)

I, John, your brother who share with you in Jesus the persecution and the kingdom and the patient endurance, was on the island called Patmos because of the word of God and the testimony of Jesus. I was in the spirit on the Lord's day, and I heard behind me a loud voice like a trumpet saying, "Write in a book what you see and send it to the seven Churches."

Then I turned to see whose voice it was that spoke to me, and on turning I saw seven golden lampstands, and in the midst of the lampstands I saw one like the Son of Man, clothed with a long robe and with a golden sash across his chest.

When I saw him, I fell at his feet as though dead. But he placed his right hand on me, saying, "Do not be afraid; I am the first and the last, and the living one. I was dead, but see, I am alive forever and ever; and I have the keys of Death and of Hades. Now write what you have seen, what is, and what is to take place after this."

The word of the Lord. Thanks be to God.

A reading from the holy Gospel according to John
(20.19-31)

It was evening on the day Jesus rose from the dead, the first day of the week, and the doors of the house where the disciples had met were locked for fear of the Jews. Jesus came and stood among them and said, "Peace be with you." After he said this, he showed them his hands and his side. Then the disciples rejoiced when they saw the Lord. Jesus said to them again, "Peace be with you. As the Father has sent me, so I send you."

When he had said this, he breathed on them and said to them, "Receive the Holy Spirit. If you forgive the sins of any, they are forgiven them; if you retain the sins of any, they are retained."

But Thomas, who was called the Twin, one of the twelve, was not with them when Jesus came. So the other disciples told him, "We have seen the Lord." But he said to them, "Unless I see the mark of the nails in his hands, and put my finger in the mark of the nails and my hand in his side, I will not believe."

After eight days his disciples were again in the house, and Thomas was with them. Although the doors were shut, Jesus came and stood among them and said, "Peace be with you." Then he said to Thomas, "Put your finger here and see my hands. Reach out your hand and put it in my side. Do not doubt but believe." Thomas answered him, "My Lord and my God!"

Jesus said to him, "Have you believed because you have seen me? Blessed are those who have not seen and yet have come to believe."

Now Jesus did many other signs in the presence of his disciples, which are not written in this book. But these are written so that you may come to believe that Jesus is the Christ, the Son of God, and that through believing you may have life in his name.

The Gospel of the Lord.
Praise to you,
Lord Jesus Christ.

During the Easter season, the first reading in the Sunday Mass is taken from the New Testament book of the Acts of the Apostles. This book relates how God went about forming the first Christian communities after the resurrection of Jesus.

Solomon's Portico or doorway was in the great atrium of the temple in Jerusalem. It was the entrance to the area where only the Jews could be present.

There were a great number of conversions to Christianity in the first years after the resurrection of Jesus. They were all cured is a sign of the miracles that were performed. The early Church shared in the power that Jesus showed towards people who were suffering.

Revelation is the last book of the Bible. It is written in a very symbolic way. Everything has a meaning: the colours, the numbers, the animals, even the monsters. These stories helped Christians who were being persecuted, so that they wouldn't be discouraged in the face of difficulties.

A person who experiences a strong feeling of peace when deep in prayer can be said to be in the spirit. For a few moments, this person may be deeply in God's presence, where nothing can distract them.

The Son of Man in the reading from Revelation is Jesus resurrected. This is one of the many names given to the Messiah. The long robe and sash that he wears are signs of his importance.

By showing his hands and his side, Jesus presented the scars left by the nails and the lance that pierced his chest. It is a way of saying, "It's me. I was dead, but now I am alive."

When Jesus says, "Blessed are those who have not seen and yet have come to believe," we can imagine he is speaking to us. Jesus walked the earth over two thousand years ago, and yet we believe in him without having seen him.

April 14

3rd Sunday of Easter

A reading from the Acts of the Apostles (5.28-32, 40-41)

In those days: The high priest questioned the Apostles, saying, "We gave you strict orders not to teach in this name, yet here you have filled Jerusalem with your teaching and you are determined to bring this man's blood on us."

But Peter and the Apostles answered, "We must obey God rather than human beings. The God of our ancestors raised up Jesus, whom you had killed by hanging him on a tree. God exalted him at his right hand as Leader and Saviour that he might give repentance to Israel and forgiveness of sins. And we are witnesses to these things, and so is the Holy Spirit whom God has given to those who obey him."

Then the council ordered the Apostles not to speak in the name of Jesus, and let them go. As they left the council, they rejoiced that they were considered worthy to suffer dishonour for the sake of the name.

The word of the Lord. **Thanks be to God.**

Psalm 30

R. **I will extol you, Lord, for you have raised me up.**

or **Alleluia!**

I will extol you, O Lord, for you have drawn me up,
and did not let my foes rejoice over me.
O Lord, you brought up my soul from Sheol,
restored me to life from among those gone down
　　to the Pit. R.

Sing praises to the Lord, O you his faithful ones,
and give thanks to his holy name.
For his anger is but for a moment;
his favour is for a lifetime.
Weeping may linger for the night,
but joy comes with the morning. R.

Hear, O Lord, and be gracious to me!
O Lord, be my helper!
You have turned my mourning into dancing.
O Lord my God, I will give thanks to you forever. R.

A reading from the book of Revelation (5.11-14)

I, John, looked, and I heard the voice of many Angels surrounding the throne and the living creatures and the elders; they numbered myriads of myriads and thousands of thousands, singing with full voice, "Worthy is the Lamb that was slaughtered to receive power and wealth and wisdom and might and honour and glory and blessing!"

Then I heard every creature in heaven and on earth and under the earth and in the sea, and all that is in them, singing, "To the one seated on the throne and to the Lamb be blessing and honour and glory and might forever and ever!" And the four living creatures said, "Amen!" And the elders fell down and worshipped.

The word of the Lord. **Thanks be to God.**

A reading from the holy Gospel according to John (21.1-19)

Jesus showed himself again to the disciples by the Sea of Tiberias; and he showed himself in this way. Gathered there together were Simon Peter, Thomas called the Twin, Nathanael of Cana in Galilee, the sons of Zebedee, and two others of his disciples. Simon Peter said to them, "I am going fishing." They said to him, "We will go with you." They went out and got into the boat, but that night they caught nothing.

Just after daybreak, Jesus stood on the beach; but the disciples did not know that it was Jesus. Jesus said to them, "Children, you have no fish, have you?" They answered him, "No." He said to them, "Cast the net to the right side of the boat, and you will find some." So they cast it, and now they were not able to haul it in because there were so many fish.

That disciple whom Jesus loved said to Peter, "It is the Lord!" When Simon Peter heard that it was the Lord, he put on some clothes, for he was naked, and jumped into the sea. But the other disciples came in the boat, dragging the net full of fish, for they were not far from the land, only about ninety metres off.

When they had gone ashore, they saw a charcoal fire there, with fish on it, and bread. Jesus said to them, "Bring some of the fish that you have just caught." So Simon Peter went aboard and hauled the net ashore, full of large fish, a hundred fifty-three of them; and though there were so many, the net was not torn. Jesus said to them, "Come and have breakfast." Now none of the disciples dared to ask him, "Who are you?" because they knew it was the Lord. Jesus came and took the bread and gave it to them, and did the same with the fish. This was now the third time that Jesus appeared to the disciples after he was raised from the dead.

When they had finished breakfast, Jesus said to Simon Peter, "Simon son of John, do you love me more than these?" He said to him, "Yes, Lord; you know that I love you." Jesus said to him, "Feed my lambs."

A second time he said to him, "Simon son of John, do you love me?" He said to him, "Yes, Lord; you know that I love you." Jesus said to him, "Tend my sheep."

He said to him the third time, "Simon son of John, do you love me?" Peter felt hurt because he said to him the third time, "Do you love me?" And he said to him, "Lord, you know everything; you know that I love you." Jesus said to him, "Feed my sheep. Very truly, I tell you, when you were younger, you used to fasten your own belt and to go wherever you wished. But when you grow old, you will stretch out your hands, and someone else will fasten a belt around you and take you where you do not wish to go." (He said this to indicate the kind of death by which he would glorify God.)

After this he said to him, "Follow me."

The Gospel of the Lord. **Praise to you, Lord Jesus Christ.**

To say that God exalted Jesus is to say that he raised him, elevated him and resurrected him. Jesus is the first-born of all creation.

The council was the most important group of Jews at the time of Jesus. It was a group of elders and wise men who discussed religious matters and who judged criminals.

When we extol someone, we praise them with great enthusiasm. The Psalmist has known sadness and danger in his life, but God has turned his "mourning into dancing"! For this reason, the Psalmist extols God, his power and his goodness.

The Lamb is a representation of Jesus. In the Jewish tradition, the people offered God a sacrifice of different animals, including both young and adult sheep. Because Jesus' sacrifice reconciled us to God, he is called the Lamb of God in the Bible.

Amen is a Hebrew word that means "Yes," "I agree," "I promise." It is a powerful word!

In the Gospel according to John, the apostle John who wrote the Gospel refers to himself as the disciple whom Jesus loved. When he was on the Cross, Jesus asked this same beloved apostle to take care of Mary, his mother. John then took Mary into his own home.

When Jesus told Peter to "feed my lambs," he was naming Peter to leadership of the community (today the person with this responsibility is the Pope, the successor of Peter). Jesus was also showing how this leadership was to be exercised — with the same tender care a shepherd uses to care for his sheep.

On the day that Jesus was arrested and crucified, Peter, afraid that he would also be arrested, said once, twice, and then a third time that he didn't know Jesus. After the resurrection, Jesus asked Peter three times if he truly loved him, and Peter responded "yes." His three denials were replaced by three acceptances.

April 21

4th Sunday of Easter

Paul and Barnabas went on from Perga and came to Antioch in Pisidia. On the Sabbath day they went into the synagogue and sat down.

When the meeting of the synagogue broke up, many Jews and devout converts to Judaism followed Paul and Barnabas, who spoke to them and urged them to continue in the grace of God.

The next Sabbath almost the whole city gathered to hear the word of the Lord. But when the Jewish officials saw the crowds, they were filled with jealousy; and blaspheming, they contradicted what was spoken by Paul.

Then both Paul and Barnabas spoke out boldly, saying, "It was necessary that the word of God should be spoken first to you. Since you reject it and judge yourselves to be unworthy of eternal life, we are now turning to the Gentiles. For so the Lord has commanded us, saying, 'I have set you to be a light for the Gentiles, so that you may bring salvation to the ends of the earth.'" When the Gentiles heard this, they were glad and praised the word of the Lord; and as many as had been destined for eternal life became believers.

Thus the word of the Lord spread throughout the region. But the officials incited the devout women of high standing and the leading men of the city, and stirred up persecution against Paul and Barnabas, and drove them out of their region. So they shook the dust off their feet in protest against them, and went to Iconium. And the disciples were filled with joy and with the Holy Spirit.

The word of the Lord. **Thanks be to God.**

Psalm 100

R. **We are his people: the sheep of his pasture.**
or **Alleluia!**

Make a joyful noise to the Lord, all the earth.
Worship the Lord with gladness;
come into his presence with singing. R.

Know that the Lord is God.
It is he that made us, and we are his;
we are his people, and the sheep of his pasture. R̰

For the Lord is good;
his steadfast love endures forever,
and his faithfulness to all generations. R̰

A reading from the book of Revelation (7.9, 14-17)

After this I, John, looked, and there was a great multitude that no one could count, from every nation, from all tribes and peoples and languages, standing before the throne and before the Lamb, robed in white, with palm branches in their hands. And one of the elders then said to me, "These are they who have come out of the great ordeal; they have washed their robes and made them white in the blood of the Lamb.

"For this reason they are before the throne of God, and worship him day and night within his temple, and the one who is seated on the throne will shelter them. They will hunger no more, and thirst no more; the sun will not strike them, nor any scorching heat; for the Lamb at the centre of the throne will be their shepherd, and he will guide them to springs of the water of life, and God will wipe away every tear from their eyes."

The word of the Lord. **Thanks be to God.**

A reading from the holy Gospel according to John (10.27-30)

Jesus said: "My sheep hear my voice. I know them, and they follow me. I give them eternal life, and they will never perish. No one will snatch them out of my hand. What my Father has given me is greater than all else, and no one can snatch it out of the Father's hand. The Father and I are one."

The Gospel of the Lord. **Praise to you, Lord Jesus Christ.**

Barnabas was a generous Christian. When Saul (Saint Paul) converted to Christianity, Barnabas introduced Paul to the apostles in Jerusalem, and later travelled with Paul during his long apostolic journeys.

Converts are people who have come to believe in a new religion. In the early Church, some believers converted to Judaism and then became followers of Jesus.

For some time, Christianity was not seen as a different religion from Judaism. Only when difficulties arose and the Jewish officials contradicted Paul were these religions seen as separate.

Gentiles was a term that referred to all people who were not followers of the Jewish religion.

The Hebrew word "**Alleluia**" means "praise to God — let us give thanks!" On Easter Sunday when we celebrate the resurrection of Jesus, and throughout the Easter season, we sing and say this word frequently at Mass.

The **Psalmist** calls us the sheep of his pasture to remind us that God loves and cares for us just as a shepherd loves and cares for his sheep. Nothing can take us from the care of God.

In the book of Revelation, if someone carried **palm branches** in their hands it meant that the person would die a martyr's death. For this reason, the statues of martyrs often show the saints carrying a palm branch in their hand.

5th Sunday of Easter

A reading from the Acts of the Apostles (14.21-27)

Paul and Barnabas returned to Lystra, then on to Iconium and Antioch. There they strengthened the souls of the disciples and encouraged them to continue in the faith, saying, "It is through many persecutions that we must enter the kingdom of God." And after they had appointed elders for them in each Church, with prayer and fasting they entrusted them to the Lord in whom they had come to believe.

Then they passed through Pisidia and came to Pamphylia. When they had spoken the word in Perga, they went down to Attalia. From there they sailed back to Antioch, where they had been commended to the grace of God for the work that they had completed.

When they arrived, they called the Church together and related all that God had done with them, and how he had opened a door of faith for the Gentiles.

The word of the Lord. **Thanks be to God.**

Psalm 145

R. I will bless your name for ever, my king and my God.

or Alleluia!

The Lord is gracious and merciful,
slow to anger and abounding in steadfast love.
The Lord is good to all,
and his compassion is over all that he has made. R.

All your works shall give thanks to you, O Lord,
and all your faithful shall bless you.
They shall speak of the glory of your kingdom,
and tell of your power. R.

To make known to human beings your mighty deeds,
and the glorious splendour of your kingdom.
Your kingdom is an everlasting kingdom,
and your dominion endures throughout all generations. R.

A reading from the book of Revelation (21.1-5)

Then I, John, saw a new heaven and a new earth; for the first heaven and the first earth had passed away, and the sea was no more.

And I saw the holy city, the new Jerusalem, coming down out of heaven from God, prepared as a bride adorned for her husband.

And I heard a loud voice from the throne saying, "See, the home of God is among humans. He will dwell with them as their God; they will be his peoples, and God himself will be with them; he will wipe every tear from their eyes. Death will be no more; mourning and crying and pain will be no more, for the first things have passed away." And the one who was seated on the throne said, "See, I am making all things new."

The word of the Lord. **Thanks be to God.**

A reading from the holy Gospel according to John
(13.1, 31-33, 34-35)

Before the festival of the Passover, Jesus knew that his hour had come to depart from this world and go to the Father. Having loved his own who were in the world, he loved them to the end.

During the supper, when Judas had gone out, Jesus said, "Now the Son of Man has been glorified, and God has been glorified in him. If God has been glorified in him, God will also glorify him in himself and will glorify him at once.

"Little children, I am with you only a little longer. I give you a new commandment, that you love one another. Just as I have loved you, you also should love one another. By this everyone will know that you are my disciples, if you have love for one another."

The Gospel of the Lord. **Praise to you, Lord Jesus Christ.**

155

The apostles looked for wise men or elders to help strengthen the faith life of the Christian communities. In today's Church the priests collaborate with the bishops to play this role.

The book of Revelation speaks of the Church as the new Jerusalem, the new people of God, the new kingdom of peace.

The Last Supper, where Jesus met with his disciples to celebrate the Passover, is the supper referred to here. Jesus washed his friends' feet, and, in breaking bread and sharing wine, he left us the Eucharist — his presence that we still celebrate today.

Because he knew what lay before him, Jesus was able to say that he would be glorified. Jesus' suffering and then his death were not the end. His resurrection and triumph over death opened the way for us to enter into heaven.

Through Moses, God gave us the Ten Commandments. Without changing these, God gave us a new commandment through Jesus. This most important commandment is to love one another as Jesus loved us.

Jesus desires that everyone will know who Christians are by the way we love one another. Not by our clothes, or our names, but by the way we live. This is our daily challenge!

6th Sunday of Easter

Certain individuals came down from Judea and were teaching the brothers, "Unless you are circumcised according to the custom of Moses, you cannot be saved." And after Paul and Barnabas had no small dissension and debate with them, Paul and Barnabas and some of the others were appointed to go up to Jerusalem to discuss this question with the Apostles and the elders.

Then the Apostles and the elders, with the consent of the whole Church, decided to choose men from among their members and to send them to Antioch with Paul and Barnabas. They sent Judas called Barsabbas, and Silas, leaders among the brothers, with the following letter:

"The brothers, both the Apostles and the elders, to the believers of Gentile origin in Antioch and Syria and Cilicia, greetings. Since we have heard that certain persons who have gone out from us, though with no instructions from us, have said things to disturb you and have unsettled your minds, we have decided unanimously to choose representatives and send them to you, along with our beloved Barnabas and Paul, who have risked their lives for the sake of our Lord Jesus Christ. We have therefore sent Judas and Silas, who themselves will tell you the same things by word of mouth.

"For it has seemed good to the Holy Spirit and to us to impose on you no further burden than these essentials: that you abstain from what has been sacrificed to idols, and from blood and from what is strangled, and from fornication. If you keep yourselves from these, you will do well. Farewell."

The word of the Lord. **Thanks be to God.**

R̰. Let the peoples praise you, O God;
let all the peoples praise you.

or Alleluia!

May God be gracious to us and bless us
and make his face to shine upon us,
that your way may be known upon earth,
your saving power among all nations. R̰.

Let the nations be glad and sing for joy,
for you judge the peoples with equity
and guide the nations upon earth.
Let the peoples praise you, O God;
let all the peoples praise you. R̰.

The earth has yielded its increase;
God, our God, has blessed us.
May God continue to bless us;
let all the ends of the earth revere him. R̰.

A reading from the book of Revelation (21.10-14, 22-23)

In the spirit the Angel carried me away to a great, high mountain and showed me the holy city Jerusalem coming down out of heaven from God. It has the glory of God and a radiance like a very rare jewel, like jasper, clear as crystal.

It has a great, high wall with twelve gates, and at the gates twelve Angels, and on the gates are inscribed the names of the twelve tribes of the children of Israel; on the east there were three gates, on the north three gates, on the south three gates, and on the west three gates. And the wall of the city has twelve foundations, and on them are the twelve names of the twelve Apostles of the Lamb.

I saw no temple in the city, for its temple is the Lord God the Almighty and the Lamb. And the city has no need of sun or moon to shine on it, for the glory of God is its light, and its lamp is the Lamb.

The word of the Lord. **Thanks be to God.**

Jesus said to his disciples: "Whoever loves me will keep my word, and my Father will love him, and we will come to him and make our home with him. Whoever does not love me does not keep my words; and the word that you hear is not mine, but is from the Father who sent me.

"I have said these things to you while I am still with you. But the Advocate, the Holy Spirit, whom the Father will send in my name, will teach you everything, and remind you of all that I have said to you.

"Peace I leave with you; my peace I give to you. I do not give to you as the world gives. Do not let your hearts be troubled, and do not let them be afraid.

"You heard me say to you, 'I am going away, and I am coming to you.' If you loved me, you would rejoice that I am going to the Father, because the Father is greater than I. And now I have told you this before it occurs, so that when it does occur, you may believe."

The Gospel of the Lord.
**Praise to you,
Lord Jesus Christ.**

This dissension in the early Church was a disagreement over whether people who were not followers of the Jewish law could become Christians. Paul and Barnabas felt that God's love was available to all through membership in the Christian community, and that new Christians did not need to become Jewish first.

In the Acts of the Apostles, we read about the disciples trying to decide whether non-Jewish followers of Jesus had to follow all the Jewish laws in order to join the Church. In the end, after much discussion, the Holy Spirit led them to decide to ease the burden or heavy load for new followers by settling on a few laws.

When we say someone is gracious, we usually mean they are kind and courteous. But when we say God is gracious, we mean God is the overflowing source of grace.

The writer of the book of Revelation saw the holy city Jerusalem as resplendently beautiful because its people had been united to God by following Jesus and his teachings.

When the book of Revelation speaks of the twelve tribes of Israel, it means the whole history of these people until Jesus came. When it speaks of the twelve apostles, it refers to all that happened in the life of the Christian Church. So here the number twelve means all the Old Testament or Hebrew Scriptures and all the New Testament or Christian Scriptures.

When Jesus and his Father find a person who lives a holy life, they say they will make our home with them. God will remain close to the person who loves God, so close that God dwells right within them.

After Jesus ascended to heaven, the Church had the power to carry on. The words of Jesus will not be forgotten because the Holy Spirit will help us remember all that Jesus taught and give us the strength to live faithfully.

May 12

Ascension of the Lord

In the first book, Theophilus, I wrote about all that Jesus did and taught from the beginning until the day when he was taken up to heaven, after giving instructions through the Holy Spirit to the Apostles whom he had chosen. After his suffering he presented himself alive to them by many convincing proofs, appearing to them during forty days and speaking about the kingdom of God.

While staying with them, he ordered them not to leave Jerusalem, but to wait there for the promise of the Father. "This," he said, "is what you have heard from me; for John baptized with water, but you will be baptized with the Holy Spirit not many days from now."

So when they had come together, they asked him, "Lord, is this the time when you will restore the kingdom to Israel?" He replied, "It is not for you to know the times or periods that the Father has set by his own authority. But you will receive power when the Holy Spirit has come upon you; and you will be my witnesses in Jerusalem, in all Judea and Samaria, and to the ends of the earth."

When he had said this, as they were watching, he was lifted up, and a cloud took him out of their sight. While he was going and they were gazing up toward heaven, suddenly two men in white robes stood by them. They said, "Men of Galilee, why do you stand looking up toward heaven? This Jesus, who has been taken up from you into heaven, will come in the same way as you saw him go into heaven."

The word of the Lord. **Thanks be to God.**

Psalm 47

R. **God has gone up with a shout,**
the Lord with the sound of a trumpet.

or **Alleluia!**

Clap your hands, all you peoples;
shout to God with loud songs of joy.
For the Lord, the Most High, is awesome,
a great king over all the earth. R.

God has gone up with a shout,
the Lord with the sound of a trumpet.
Sing praises to God, sing praises;
sing praises to our King, sing praises. R.

For God is the king of all the earth;
sing praises with a Psalm.
God is king over the nations;
God sits on his holy throne. R.

An alternate reading follows.

A reading from the Letter of Saint Paul to the Ephesians   (1.17-23)

Brothers and sisters: I pray that the God of our Lord Jesus Christ, the Father of glory, may give you a spirit of wisdom and revelation as you come to know him, so that, with the eyes of your heart enlightened, you may know what is the hope to which he has called you, what are the riches of his glorious inheritance among the saints, and what is the immeasurable greatness of his power for us who believe, according to the working of his great power.

God put this power to work in Christ when he raised him from the dead and seated him at his right hand in the heavenly places, far above all rule and authority and power and dominion, and above every name that is named, not only in this age but also in the age to come.

And he has put all things under his feet and has made him the head over all things for the Church, which is his body, the fullness of him who fills all in all.

The word of the Lord. **Thanks be to God.**

or

A reading from the Letter to the Hebrews
(9.24-28; 10.19-23)

Christ did not enter a sanctuary made by human hands, a mere copy of the true one, but he entered into heaven itself, now to appear in the presence of God on our behalf. Nor was it to offer himself again and again, as the high priest enters the Holy Place year after year with blood that is not his own; for then he would have had to suffer again and again since the foundation of the world. But as it is, he has appeared once for all at the end of the age to remove sin by the sacrifice of himself.

And just as it is appointed for human beings to die once, and after that comes the judgment, so Christ, having been offered once to bear the sins of many, will appear a second time, not to deal with sin, but to save those who are eagerly waiting for him.

Therefore, brothers and sisters, since we have confidence to enter the sanctuary by the blood of Jesus, by the new and living way that he opened for us through the curtain, that is, through his flesh, and since we have a great priest over the house of God, let us approach with a true heart in full assurance of faith, with our hearts sprinkled clean from an evil conscience and our bodies washed with pure water. Let us hold fast to the confession of our hope without wavering, for he who has promised is faithful.

The word of the Lord. **Thanks be to God.**

Jesus said to the disciples, "These are my words that I spoke to you while I was still with you — that everything written about me in the Law of Moses, the Prophets, and the Psalms must be fulfilled."

Then he opened their minds to understand the Scriptures, and he said to them, "Thus it is written, that the Christ is to suffer and to rise from the dead on the third day, and that repentance and forgiveness of sins is to be proclaimed in his name to all nations, beginning from Jerusalem. You are witnesses of these things.

"And see, I am sending upon you what my Father promised; so stay here in the city until you have been clothed with power from on high."

Then he led them out as far as Bethany, and, lifting up his hands, he blessed them. While he was blessing them, he withdrew from them and was carried up into heaven. And they worshipped him, and returned to Jerusalem with great joy; and they were continually in the temple blessing God.

The Gospel of the Lord.
**Praise to you,
Lord Jesus Christ.**

Saint Luke, the author of the Acts of the Apostles, also wrote a Gospel. The first book he refers to here is that Gospel. The Gospel of Luke tells us what Jesus did, what he taught, and how he died and rose from the dead. The second book, the Acts of the Apostles, describes the first years of the life of the Church and the early Christian communities.

In the Bible, the expression "kingdom of God" describes a way of living as God asks. To enter into the kingdom means to live as children of God. The disciples, however, thought that Jesus was going to restore the independence of the Jews, releasing them from the Roman kingdom and setting up a earthly kingdom for the Jews.

The Ascension of the Lord celebrates the day when Christ was lifted up to heaven, forty days after his resurrection. Jesus is still with us in spirit, but his resurrected body is with God.

The Hebrew word "Alleluia" means "praise to God — we must give thanks!" On Easter Sunday when we celebrate the resurrection of Jesus, and throughout the Easter season, we sing and say this word frequently at Mass.

A sanctuary made by human hands is a holy place of safety and rest. In some religions, only very holy people and priests can enter the sanctuary of a church or temple. Jesus entered the holiest of sanctuaries, heaven itself.

The confession of our hope is our faith in Jesus, especially our hope that he calls us to live with him in the kingdom of heaven, to enjoy everlasting life.

After Jesus ascended to heaven, the principal mission of the apostles was to be witnesses of the death and resurrection of Jesus. This remains the task of the followers of Christ today.

May 19

Pentecost Sunday

A reading from the Acts of the Apostles (2.1-11)

When the day of Pentecost had come, they were all together in one place. And suddenly from heaven there came a sound like the rush of a violent wind, and it filled the entire house where they were sitting. Divided tongues, as of fire, appeared among them, and a tongue rested on each of them. All of them were filled with the Holy Spirit and began to speak in other languages, as the Spirit gave them ability.

Now there were devout Jews from every nation under heaven living in Jerusalem. And at this sound the crowd gathered and was bewildered, because each one heard them speaking in their own language. Amazed and astonished, they asked, "Are not all these who are speaking Galileans? And how is it that we hear, each of us, in our own language? Parthians, Medes, Elamites, and residents of Mesopotamia, Judea and Cappadocia, Pontus and Asia, Phrygia and Pamphylia, Egypt and the parts of Libya belonging to Cyrene, and visitors from Rome, both Jews and converts, Cretans and Arabs — in our own languages we hear them speaking about God's deeds of power."

The word of the Lord. **Thanks be to God.**

Psalm 104

R. **Lord, send forth your Spirit,
and renew the face of the earth.**

or **Alleluia!**

Bless the Lord, O my soul.
O Lord my God, you are very great.
O Lord, how manifold are your works!
The earth is full of your creatures. R.

When you take away their breath,
they die and return to their dust.
When you send forth your spirit, they are created;
and you renew the face of the earth. R.

May the glory of the Lord endure forever;
may the Lord rejoice in his works.
May my meditation be pleasing to him,
for I rejoice in the Lord. R.

An alternate reading follows.

A reading from the first Letter of Saint Paul to the Corinthians (12.3-7, 12-13)

Brothers and sisters: No one can say "Jesus is Lord" except by the Holy Spirit.

Now there are varieties of gifts, but the same Spirit; and there are varieties of services, but the same Lord; and there are varieties of activities, but it is the same God who activates all of them in everyone. To each is given the manifestation of the Spirit for the common good.

For just as the body is one and has many members, and all the members of the body, though many, are one body, so it is with Christ. For in the one Spirit we were all baptized into one body — Jews or Greeks, slaves or free — and we were all made to drink of one Spirit.

The word of the Lord. **Thanks be to God.**

or

A reading from the Letter of Saint Paul to the Romans (8.8-17)

Brothers and sisters: Those who are in the flesh cannot please God. But you are not in the flesh; you are in the Spirit, since the Spirit of God dwells in you. Anyone who does not have the Spirit of Christ does not belong to him.

But if Christ is in you, though the body is dead because of sin, the Spirit is life because of righteousness. If the Spirit of God who raised Jesus from the dead dwells in you, he who raised Christ from the dead will give life to your mortal bodies also through his Spirit that dwells in you.

So then, brothers and sisters, we are debtors, not to the flesh, to live according to the flesh — for if you live according to the flesh, you will die; but if by the Spirit you put to death the deeds of the body, you will live. For all who are led by the Spirit of God are sons and daughters of God. For you did not receive a spirit of slavery to fall back into fear, but you have received a spirit of adoption to sonship. When we cry, "Abba! Father!" it is that very Spirit bearing witness with our spirit that we are children of God, and if children, then heirs, heirs of God and joint heirs with Christ — if, in fact, we suffer with him so that we may also be glorified with him.

The word of the Lord. **Thanks be to God.**

An alternate Gospel follows.

A reading from the holy Gospel according to John
(20.19-23)

It was evening on the day Jesus rose from the dead, the first day of the week, and the doors of the house where the disciples had met were locked for fear of the Jews. Jesus came and stood among them and said, "Peace be with you." After he said this, he showed them his hands and his side. Then the disciples rejoiced when they saw the Lord.

Jesus said to them again, "Peace be with you. As the Father has sent me, so I send you."

When he had said this, he breathed on them and said to them, "Receive the Holy Spirit. If you forgive the sins of any, they are forgiven them; if you retain the sins of any, they are retained."

The Gospel of the Lord. **Praise to you, Lord Jesus Christ.**

or

A reading from the holy Gospel according to John
(14.15-16, 23-26)

Jesus said to the disciples: "If you love me, you will keep my commandments. And I will ask the Father, and he will give you another Advocate, to be with you forever.

"Whoever loves me will keep my word, and my Father will love him, and we will come to him and make our home with him. Whoever does not love me does not keep my words; and the word that you hear is not mine, but is from the Father who sent me.

"I have said these things to you while I am still with you. But the Advocate, the Holy Spirit, whom the Father will send in my name, will teach you everything, and remind you of all that I have said to you."

The Gospel of the Lord. **Praise to you, Lord Jesus Christ.**

Pentecost is the Greek word for a Jewish festival that takes place on the fiftieth day after Passover. Fifty days after Jesus' resurrection, the Holy Spirit descended upon all those present in the upper room of a house. For Christians, Pentecost is the feast of the coming of the Holy Spirit and the birthday of the Church.

The Holy Spirit, the third person of the Trinity, is always with the Church in order to help us live better. We receive the Holy Spirit in baptism as God's great gift.

Meditation is a form of prayer that is silent, still and very profound. It brings us close to God who dwells within us. God speaks to us in the silence.

When we live in the flesh, we live in a way totally opposite to living in the Spirit. To live in the flesh is to make comfort, ease and wealth our priority. To live in the Spirit is to follow Jesus and love our neighbour as ourselves.

Christians know that we are children of God. Since God is our parent, then all other human beings are our brothers and sisters.

The Advocate is another name for the Holy Spirit, sent by Jesus to be our helper and guide until the end of time.

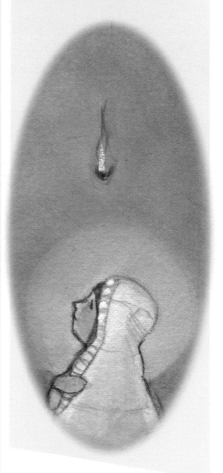

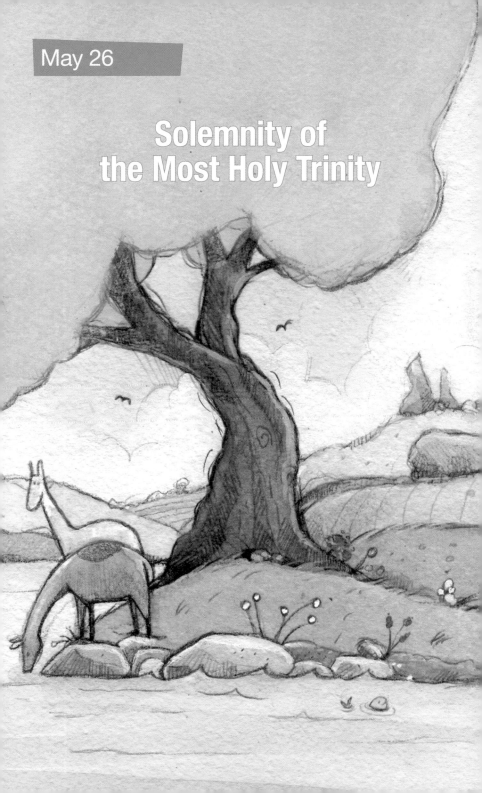

May 26

Solemnity of
the Most Holy Trinity

Thus says the Wisdom of God:

"The Lord created me at the beginning of his work,
the first of his acts of long ago.
Ages ago I was set up,
at the first, before the beginning of the earth.
When there were no depths I was brought forth,
when there were no springs abounding with water.

"Before the mountains had been shaped,
before the hills, I was brought forth —
when he had not yet made earth and fields,
or the world's first bits of soil.

"When he established the heavens, I was there,
when he drew a circle on the face of the deep,
when he made firm the skies above,
when he established the fountains of the deep,
when he assigned to the sea its limit,
so that the waters might not transgress his command,
when he marked out the foundations of the earth,
then I was beside him, like a master worker;
and I was daily his delight,
rejoicing before him always,
rejoicing in his inhabited world
and delighting in the children of Adam."

The word of the Lord. **Thanks be to God.**

Psalm 8

℟ **O Lord, our God, how majestic is your name in all the earth!**

When I look at your heavens, the work of your fingers,
the moon and the stars that you have established;
what is a man that you are mindful of him,
or the son of man that you care for him? ℟

Yet you have made him a little lower than the Angels,
and crowned him with glory and honour.
You have given him dominion over the works of your hands;
you have put all things under his feet. ℟

All sheep and oxen,
and also the beasts of the field,
the birds of the air, and the fish of the sea,
whatever passes along the paths of the seas. R.

A reading from the Letter of Saint Paul to the Romans (5.1-5)

Brothers and sisters: Since we are justified by faith, we have peace with God through our Lord Jesus Christ, through whom we have obtained access to this grace in which we stand; and we boast in our hope of sharing the glory of God.

And not only that, but we also boast in our sufferings, knowing that suffering produces endurance, and endurance produces character, and character produces hope, and hope does not disappoint us, because God's love has been poured into our hearts through the Holy Spirit that has been given to us.

The word of the Lord. **Thanks be to God.**

A reading from the holy Gospel according to John (16.12-15)

Jesus said to his disciples: "I still have many things to say to you, but you cannot bear them now. When the Spirit of truth comes, he will guide you into all the truth; for he will not speak on his own, but will speak whatever he hears, and he will declare to you the things that are to come. He will glorify me, because he will take what is mine and declare it to you. All that the Father has is mine. For this reason I said that he will take what is mine and declare it to you."

The Gospel of the Lord. **Praise to you, Lord Jesus Christ.**

The book of Proverbs is found in the oldest part of the Bible called the Old Testament. It is a collection of popular sayings and expressions of knowledge assembled over many centuries.

The children of Adam is another way of speaking about all human beings. Adam was the first person, and so we are all descendants or children of Adam.

The Letter of Saint Paul to the Romans is the longest surviving letter that Saint Paul wrote. The Christians who lived in Rome belonged to a small community. Paul planned to travel to preach in Spain, and on the way to stop in Rome to visit the Christians. He sent this letter ahead in order to encourage them and to remind them of the teachings of Jesus.

Because we have real faith, we can boast of or take pride in even the most intense sufferings, because through them we could come to experience a greater closeness to God.

Jesus spent much time teaching about the kingdom of God by his words, his miracles and, above all, through his death and resurrection. But when he was ready to say goodbye to his disciples, he realized that they had not understood, and could not bear to understand, everything Jesus had to tell them. The same thing happens to us: we need to continue to try to understand the teachings of Jesus.

The Spirit of truth is the Holy Spirit, present and working in the Church so that we may better understand and remember all that Jesus taught.

Solemnity of the Most Holy Body and Blood of Christ

A reading from the book of Genesis (14.18-20)

In those days: After Abram's return King Melchizedek of Salem brought out bread and wine; he was priest of God Most High. He blessed Abram and said, "Blessed be Abram by God Most High, maker of heaven and earth; and blessed be God Most High, who has delivered your enemies into your hand!" And Abram gave him one tenth of everything.

The word of the Lord. **Thanks be to God.**

Psalm 110

R̶ **You are a priest forever,
according to the order of Melchizedek.**

The Lord says to my lord,
"Sit at my right hand
until I make your enemies your footstool." R̶

The Lord sends out from Zion
your mighty sceptre.
Rule in the midst of your foes. R̶

Your people will offer themselves willingly
on the day you lead your forces on the holy mountains.
From the womb of the morning, like dew,
your youth will come to you. R̶

The Lord has sworn and will not change his mind,
"You are a priest forever
according to the order of Melchizedek." R̶

A reading from the first Letter of Saint Paul to the Corinthians (11.23-26)

Brothers and sisters: I received from the Lord what I also handed on to you, that the Lord Jesus on the night when he was betrayed took a loaf of bread, and when he had given thanks, he broke it and said, "This is my Body that is for you. Do this in remembrance of me."

In the same way he took the cup also, after supper, saying, "This cup is the new covenant in my Blood. Do this, as often as you drink it, in remembrance of me."

For as often as you eat this bread and drink the cup, you proclaim the Lord's death until he comes.

The word of the Lord. **Thanks be to God.**

A reading from the holy Gospel according to Luke (9.11-17)

Jesus spoke to the crowds about the kingdom of God, and healed those who needed to be cured.

The day was drawing to a close, and the twelve came to him and said, "Send the crowd away, so that they may go into the surrounding villages and countryside, to lodge and get provisions; for we are here in a deserted place."

But Jesus said to them, "You give them something to eat." They said, "We have no more than five loaves and two fish — unless we are to go and buy food for all these people." For there were about five thousand men.

And Jesus said to his disciples, "Make the people sit down in groups of about fifty each." They did so and made them all sit down.

And taking the five loaves and the two fish, he looked up to heaven, and blessed and broke them, and gave them to the disciples to set before the crowd.

And all ate and were filled. What was left over was gathered up, twelve baskets of broken pieces.

The Gospel of the Lord. **Praise to you, Lord Jesus Christ.**

Melchizedek was a holy man, a priest, and a king who lived long before the time of Jesus. The fact that he worshipped God by taking bread and wine, exactly as Jesus did at the Last Supper, and as we do at the Eucharist today, shows how long God has been patiently trying to show us how to live and how to pray.

When we read that the Lord has sworn, we understand that God has made a promise that will never be broken. Even when we turn away from God, God always keeps his promise.

When we do something in remembrance of someone, we are performing an action to show our respect and affection for the person who has died.

To lodge is to sleep over somewhere that is not your own house. It would be next to impossible for five thousand people or more to find lodging on such short notice.

Jesus and the disciples fed an enormous crowd, for there were surely women and children present, in addition to the five thousand men mentioned by Saint Luke in the Gospel.

June 9

10th Sunday in Ordinary Time

In those days, the son of the woman, the mistress of the house, became ill; his illness was so severe that there was no breath left in him.

She then said to Elijah, "What have you against me, O man of God? You have come to me to bring my sins to remembrance, and to cause the death of my son!"

But Elijah said to her, "Give me your son." He took him from her bosom, carried him up into the upper chamber where he was lodging, and laid him on his own bed. Elijah cried out to the Lord, "O Lord my God, have you brought calamity even upon the widow with whom I am staying, by killing her son?" Three times he cried out to the Lord, "O Lord my God, let this child's life come into him again."

The Lord listened to the voice of Elijah; the life of the child came into him again, and he revived.

Elijah took the child, brought him down from the upper chamber into the house, and gave him to his mother; then Elijah said, "See, your son is alive."

So the woman said to Elijah, "Now I know that you are a man of God, and that the word of the Lord in your mouth is truth."

The word of the Lord. **Thanks be to God.**

Psalm 30

R. **I will extol you, Lord, for you have raised me up.**

I will extol you, O Lord, for you have drawn me up,
and did not let my foes rejoice over me.
O Lord, you brought up my soul from Sheol,
restored me to life from among those gone down to the Pit. R.

Sing praises to the Lord, O you his faithful ones,
and give thanks to his holy name.
For his anger is but for a moment;
his favour is for a lifetime.
Weeping may linger for the night,
but joy comes with the morning. R.

Hear, O Lord, and be gracious to me!
O Lord, be my helper!
You have turned my mourning into dancing.
O Lord my God, I will give thanks to you forever. ℟

A reading from the Letter of Saint Paul to the Galatians (1.11-19)

I want you to know, brothers and sisters, that the Gospel that was proclaimed by me is not of human origin; for I did not receive it from a human being, nor was I taught it, but I received it through a revelation of Jesus Christ.

You have heard, no doubt, of my earlier life in Judaism. I was violently persecuting the Church of God and was trying to destroy it. I advanced in Judaism beyond many among my people of the same age, for I was far more zealous for the traditions of my ancestors.

But when God, who had set me apart before I was born and called me through his grace, was pleased to reveal his Son to me, so that I might proclaim him among the Gentiles, I did not confer with flesh and blood, nor did I go up to Jerusalem to those who were already Apostles before me, but I went away at once into Arabia, and afterwards I returned to Damascus.

Then after three years I did go up to Jerusalem to visit Cephas and stayed with him fifteen days; but I did not see any other apostle except James the Lord's brother.

The word of the Lord. **Thanks be to God.**

Jesus went to a town called Nain, and his disciples and a large crowd went with him. As he approached the gate of the town, a man who had died was being carried out. He was his mother's only son, and she was a widow; and with her was a large crowd from the town.

When the Lord saw her, he had compassion for her and said to her, "Do not weep."

Then he came forward and touched the pallet, and the bearers stood still. And Jesus said, "Young man, I say to you, rise!" The dead man sat up and began to speak, and Jesus gave him to his mother.

Fear seized all of them; and they glorified God, saying, "A great Prophet has risen among us!" and "God has looked favourably on his people!" This word about Jesus spread throughout Judea and all the surrounding country.

The Gospel of the Lord. **Praise to you, Lord Jesus Christ.**

A widow is a woman whose husband has died. In biblical times, when a woman married she left her own family behind and relied on her husband's family for her safety and security. If a widow was left without any male family member to protect her — even a young son — then she was among the poorest of the poor. The Bible often mentions widows and orphans together as the weakest members of society; it teaches and insists that they receive special care.

Sheol is a Hebrew word that means the Pit or the grave. In biblical times, it was believed that everyone who died went to Sheol, a place of death and darkness. It is different from the later idea of Hell, for there is no judgment associated with Sheol; it is simply the place of the dead. When Jesus died, he freed the righteous souls from death or from Sheol, where they were awaiting the coming of the Messiah.

The Christians of Galatia began to get confused because some preachers were telling them that to be Christians, they first had to convert to Judaism and follow the entire Jewish law. Saint Paul wrote to the Galatians to reassure them and explain to them the importance of following Jesus' teachings.

When we learn something new, we learn it from another person: from an author of a book, an expert, a friend. In his letter to the Galatians, Saint Paul writes that he learned the Good News from Jesus the Son of God himself — not of human origin. This gives Saint Paul authority when he speaks.

Cephas is the Greek name for Peter and both names mean "rock." Saint Paul is referring to Saint Peter when he uses the name Cephas, a name which together with Peter is a version of the new name Jesus gave to Simon when he said "upon this 'rock' I will build my church."

11th Sunday in Ordinary Time

A reading from the second book of Samuel (12.7-10, 13)

David did what displeased the Lord, and the Lord sent the Prophet Nathan to David. Nathan said to David, "Thus says the Lord, the God of Israel: I anointed you king over Israel, and I rescued you from the hand of Saul; I gave you your master's house, and your master's wives into your bosom, and gave you the house of Israel and of Judah; if that had been too little, I would have added as much more.

"Why have you despised the word of the Lord, to do what is evil in his sight? You have struck down Uriah the Hittite with the sword, and have taken his wife to be your wife, and have killed Uriah with the sword of the Ammonites.

"Now therefore the sword shall never depart from your house, for you have despised me, and have taken the wife of Uriah the Hittite to be your wife."

David said to Nathan, "I have sinned against the Lord." Nathan said to David, "Now the Lord has put away your sin; you shall not die."

The word of the Lord. **Thanks be to God.**

Psalm 32

R. **Lord, forgive the guilt of my sin.**

Blessed is the one whose transgression is forgiven,
whose sin is covered.
Blessed is the one to whom the Lord imputes no iniquity,
and in whose spirit there is no deceit. R.

I acknowledged my sin to you,
and I did not hide my iniquity;
I said, "I will confess my transgressions to the Lord,"
and you forgave the guilt of my sin. R.

You are a hiding place for me;
you preserve me from trouble;
you surround me with glad cries of deliverance. R.

Be glad in the Lord and rejoice, O righteous,
and shout for joy, all you upright in heart. R.

Brothers and sisters: We know that a person is justified not by the works of the law but through faith in Jesus Christ. And we have come to believe in Christ Jesus, so that we might be justified by faith in Christ, and not by doing the works of the law, because no one will be justified by the works of the law. For through the law I died to the law, so that I might live to God.

I have been crucified with Christ; and it is no longer I who live, but it is Christ who lives in me. And the life I now live in the flesh I live by faith in the Son of God, who loved me and gave himself for me. I do not nullify the grace of God; for if justification comes through the law, then Christ died for nothing.

The word of the Lord. **Thanks be to God.**

One of the Pharisees asked Jesus to eat with him, and he went into the Pharisee's house and took his place at the table.

A woman in the city, who was a sinner, having learned that Jesus was eating in the Pharisee's house, brought an alabaster jar of ointment. She stood behind Jesus at his feet, weeping, and began to bathe his feet with her tears and to dry them with her hair. Then she continued kissing his feet and anointing them with the ointment.

Now when the Pharisee who had invited Jesus saw it, he said to himself, "If this man were a Prophet, he would have known who and what kind of woman this is who is touching him — that she is a sinner."

Jesus spoke up and said to him, "Simon, I have something to say to you." "Teacher," he replied, "speak."

"A certain creditor had two debtors; one owed five hundred denarii, and the other fifty. When they could not pay, he cancelled the debts for both of them. Now which of them will love him more?" Simon answered, "I suppose the one for whom he cancelled the greater debt." And Jesus said to him, "You have judged rightly."

Then turning toward the woman, he said to Simon, "Do you see this woman? I entered your house; you gave me no water for my feet, but she has bathed my feet with her tears and dried them with her hair.

"You gave me no kiss, but from the time I came in she has not stopped kissing my feet. You did not anoint my head with oil, but she has anointed my feet with ointment.

"Therefore, I tell you, her sins, which were many, have been forgiven; hence she has shown great love. But the one to whom little is forgiven, loves little." Then Jesus said to her, "Your sins are forgiven."

But those who were at the table with him began to say among themselves, "Who is this who even forgives sins?" And Jesus said to the woman, "Your faith has saved you; go in peace."

Soon afterwards Jesus went on through cities and villages, proclaiming and bringing the good news of the kingdom of God. The twelve were with him, as well as some women who had been cured of evil spirits and infirmities: Mary, called Magdalene, from whom seven demons had gone out, and Joanna, the wife of Herod's steward Chuza, and Susanna, and many others, who provided for them out of their resources.

The Gospel of the Lord.
**Praise to you,
Lord Jesus Christ.**

Samuel was a prophet and judge in Israel. God chose Samuel to anoint the first king of Israel, Saul. Samuel was born about 1,000 years before Christ. In the Bible there are two books that have his name: the first and second books of Samuel.

Nathan was an important prophet who strongly criticized King David when the king was not faithful to God. When David was dying, it was Nathan who encouraged David to name Solomon, David's youngest son, as his successor.

This encounter in the Bible between David and Nathan is a good example of God's great mercy toward those who repent of their sins, no matter how great. David realized with sorrow that he had sinned against the Lord, but the Prophet immediately told David that God had forgiven him.

Christians are united with Christ by our baptism. We are able to say (as did Saint Paul), "I have been crucified with Christ." More important, we have also been resurrected with him.

The Pharisees were Jews who belonged to a very strict sect, one which followed all the religious rules but sometimes forgot to live with love. They were not well liked among the common people.

At the time of Jesus, in order to welcome politely a visitor to your house, you would offer water for them to wash their feet. If no water for my feet was offered, such a visitor would not feel at ease.

"Who is this who even forgives sins?" expresses the people's wonder and admiration for Jesus, because they knew that only God can forgive sins. But when Jesus announced that he forgave the woman's sins, some people, including the Pharisees, resented Jesus and wanted to stop him from teaching.

12th Sunday in Ordinary Time

The Lord says this: "I will pour out a spirit of compassion and supplication on the house of David and the inhabitants of Jerusalem, so that, when they look on the one whom they have pierced, they shall mourn for him, as one mourns for an only-begotten son, and weep bitterly over him, as one weeps over a firstborn.

"On that day the mourning in Jerusalem will be as great as the mourning for Hadad-rimmon in the plain of Megiddo."

The word of the Lord. **Thanks be to God.**

Psalm 63

R. **My soul thirsts for you, O Lord my God.**

O God, you are my God, I seek you,
my soul thirsts for you;
my flesh faints for you,
as in a dry and weary land where there is no water. R.

So I have looked upon you in the sanctuary,
beholding your power and glory.
Because your steadfast love is better than life,
my lips will praise you. R.

So I will bless you as long as I live;
I will lift up my hands and call on your name.
My soul is satisfied as with a rich feast,
and my mouth praises you with joyful lips. R.

For you have been my help,
and in the shadow of your wings I sing for joy.
My soul clings to you;
your right hand upholds me. R.

A reading from the Letter of Saint Paul to the Galatians (3.26-29)

Brothers and sisters, in Christ Jesus you are all sons and daughters of God through faith. As many of you as were baptized into Christ have clothed yourselves with Christ.

There is no longer Jew or Greek, there is no longer slave or free, there is no longer male and female; for all of you are one in Christ Jesus.

And if you belong to Christ, then you are Abraham's offspring, heirs according to the promise.

The word of the Lord. **Thanks be to God.**

A reading from the holy Gospel according to Luke (9.18-24)

One day when Jesus was praying alone, with only the disciples near him, he asked them, "Who do the crowds say that I am?"

They answered, "John the Baptist; but others, Elijah; and still others, that one of the ancient Prophets has arisen." Jesus said to them, "But who do you say that I am?" Peter answered, "The Christ of God."

Jesus sternly ordered and commanded the disciples not to tell anyone, saying, "The Son of Man must undergo great suffering, and be rejected by the elders, chief priests, and scribes, and be killed, and on the third day be raised."

Then he said to them all, "If anyone wants to become my follower, let him deny himself and take up his cross daily and follow me. For whoever wants to save their life will lose it, and whoever loses their life for my sake will save it."

The Gospel of the Lord. **Praise to you, Lord Jesus Christ.**

Zechariah was a prophet who lived 600 years before Jesus. This friend of God expressed deep sadness because the temple in Jerusalem had been destroyed. But when the people decided to rebuild it, Zechariah was heartened that they wanted to return to God. This prophet encouraged the people to live with hope, because he announced the coming of the Messiah.

The sanctuary is a holy place within a church or temple. In some religions, only very holy people and priests can enter the sanctuary. The word comes from the Latin word *sanctus* meaning "holy."

Abraham was originally named Abram. When God made the promise to give him a large family, God changed his name to Abraham. He was also the first person to have faith in the one true God. Abraham is the father of our faith.

Christ is a Greek name meaning "the anointed one," someone designated for an important mission. Christ means the same as the Hebrew name "Messiah," that is to say, the person to whom God gave the mission of saving the world.

In the Gospels, Jesus is sometimes called the Son of Man. This title reminds us that he suffered as a human being. Yet we know that because Jesus is also the Son of God, suffering and death could not overcome him.

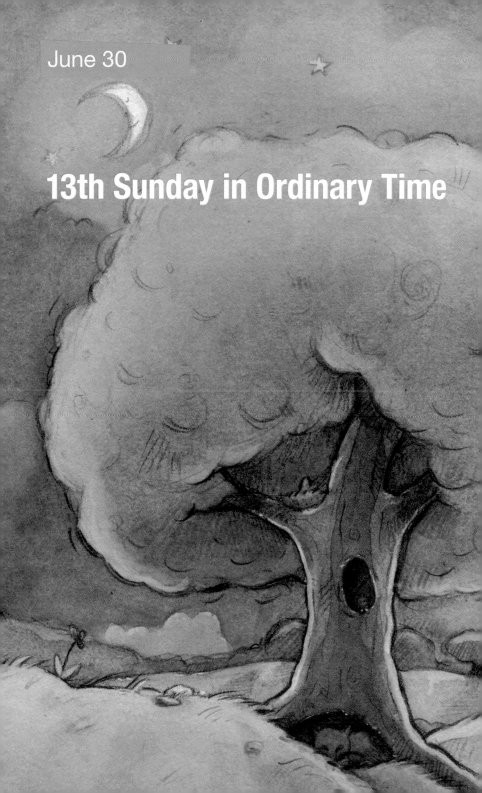

June 30

13th Sunday in Ordinary Time

A reading from the first book of Kings (19.16, 19-21)

The Lord spoke to the Prophet Elijah and said, "You shall anoint Elisha, son of Shaphat, as Prophet in your place."

So Elijah set out from there, and found Elisha, who was ploughing. There were twelve yoke of oxen ahead of him, and he was with the twelfth.

Elijah passed by Elisha and threw his mantle over him. Elisha left the oxen, ran after Elijah, and said, "Let me kiss my father and my mother, and then I will follow you."

Then Elijah said to him, "Go back again; for what have I done to you?" Elisha returned from following Elijah, took the yoke of oxen, and slaughtered them; using the equipment from the oxen, he boiled their flesh, and gave it to the people, and they ate. Then Elisha set out and followed Elijah, and became his servant.

The word of the Lord. **Thanks be to God.**

Psalm 16

R̲ **You are my chosen portion, O Lord.**

Protect me, O God, for in you I take refuge.
I say to the Lord, "You are my Lord;
I have no good apart from you."
The Lord is my chosen portion and my cup;
    you hold my lot. R̲

I bless the Lord who gives me counsel;
in the night also my heart instructs me.
I keep the Lord always before me;
    because he is at my right hand, I shall not be moved. R̲

Therefore my heart is glad, and my soul rejoices;
my body also rests secure.
For you do not give me up to Sheol,
or let your faithful one see the Pit. R̲

You show me the path of life.
In your presence there is fullness of joy;
in your right hand are pleasures forevermore. R̲

Brothers and sisters: For freedom Christ has set us free. Stand firm, therefore, and do not submit again to a yoke of slavery. For you were called to freedom, brothers and sisters; only do not use your freedom as an opportunity for self-indulgence, but through love become slaves to one another.

For the whole law is summed up in a single commandment, "You shall love your neighbour as yourself." If, however, you bite and devour one another, take care that you are not consumed by one another.

Live by the Spirit, I say, and do not gratify the desires of the flesh. For what the flesh desires is opposed to the Spirit, and what the Spirit desires is opposed to the flesh; for these are opposed to each other, to prevent you from doing what you want. But if you are led by the Spirit, you are not subject to the law.

The word of the Lord. **Thanks be to God.**

When the days drew near for him to be taken up, Jesus set his face to go to Jerusalem.

And he sent messengers ahead of him. On their way they entered a village of the Samaritans to make ready for Jesus; but the Samaritans did not receive him, because his face was set toward Jerusalem.

When his disciples James and John saw it, they said, "Lord, do you want us to command fire to come down from heaven and consume them?" But Jesus turned and rebuked them. Then they went on to another village.

As they were going along the road, someone said to him, "I will follow you wherever you go." And Jesus said to him, "Foxes have holes, and birds of the air have nests; but the Son of Man has nowhere to lay his head."

To another Jesus said, "Follow me." But he replied, "Lord, first let me go and bury my father." But Jesus said to him, "Let the dead bury their own dead; but as for you, go and proclaim the kingdom of God."

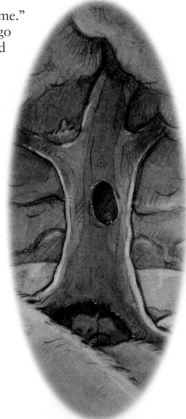

Another said, "I will follow you, Lord; but let me first say farewell to those at my home." Jesus said to him, "No one who puts a hand to the plough and looks back is fit for the kingdom of God."

The Gospel of the Lord.
Praise to you, Lord Jesus Christ.

In the Bible there are two books of Kings which together describe the era in which Israel was ruled by kings.

Elijah was a man who was very close to God. He lived in the ninth century before Christ. The Bible relates many extraordinary episodes in his life, most notably when he was taken from this world in a chariot of fire.

When someone is anointed it is a sign that they have been given an important mission for the good of the community. Oil is rubbed on that person's forehead, hands or another part of the body. We are anointed when we are baptized and confirmed; a priest is anointed when he is ordained to the priesthood; and we are anointed when we receive the sacrament of the sick.

God commanded Elijah to anoint Elisha as his successor as prophet, that is, to be the one responsible for guiding the people and keeping them from straying from their commitment to God.

Sin and death are like prisons from which we cannot escape. But Christ, with his life, death and resurrection, gave us the possibility to break out of these shackles: he set us free.

The third person of the Trinity is the Holy Spirit, who is always present in the Church and in our hearts. To live by the Spirit is to live as children of God and to live as brothers and sisters.

The ancient city of Jerusalem was the capital of Israel. The kings resided there, and Solomon constructed the magnificent temple as the centre of Jewish religious life there. Now, Jerusalem is a holy city for three great religious traditions: Christianity, Judaism and Islam.

The Samaritans did not receive Jesus because they knew he was going to Jerusalem, the holy city of Israel. The Jews and Samaritans historically did not get along, and they were forbidden from meeting or talking to each another.

14th Sunday in Ordinary Time

Rejoice with Jerusalem, and be glad for her, all you who love her;
rejoice with her in joy, all you who mourn over her —
that you may nurse and be satisfied from her consoling breast;
that you may drink deeply with delight from her glorious bosom.

For thus says the Lord:
"I will extend prosperity to her like a river,
and the wealth of the nations like an overflowing stream;
and you shall nurse and be carried on her arm,
and dandled on her knees.
As a mother comforts her child, so I will comfort you;
you shall be comforted in Jerusalem.

"You shall see, and your heart shall rejoice;
your bodies shall flourish like the grass;
and it shall be known
that the hand of the Lord is with his servants."

The word of the Lord. **Thanks be to God.**

Psalm 66

R. **Make a joyful noise to God, all the earth!**

Make a joyful noise to God, all the earth;
sing the glory of his name;
give to him glorious praise.
Say to God, "How awesome are your deeds!" R.

"All the earth worships you;
they sing praises to you, sing praises to your name."
Come and see what God has done:
he is awesome in his deeds among the children of Adam. R.

He turned the sea into dry land;
they passed through the river on foot.
There we rejoiced in him,
who rules by his might forever. R.

Come and hear, all you who fear God,
and I will tell what he has done for me.
Blessed be God, because he has not rejected my prayer
or removed his steadfast love from me. R.

A reading from the Letter of Saint Paul to the Galatians (6.14-18)

Brothers and sisters: May I never boast of anything except the Cross of our Lord Jesus Christ, by which the world has been crucified to me, and I to the world. For neither circumcision nor uncircumcision is anything; but a new creation is everything!

As for those who will follow this rule — peace be upon them, and mercy, and upon the Israel of God. From now on, let no one make trouble for me; for I carry the marks of Jesus branded on my body.

May the grace of our Lord Jesus Christ be with your spirit, brothers and sisters. Amen.

The word of the Lord. **Thanks be to God.**

A reading from the holy Gospel according to Luke (10.1-12, 17-20)

The shorter version ends at the asterisks.

The Lord appointed seventy others and sent them on ahead of him in pairs to every town and place where he himself intended to go.

He said to them, "The harvest is plentiful, but the labourers are few; therefore ask the Lord of the harvest to send out labourers into his harvest. Go on your way. See, I am sending you out like lambs into the midst of wolves. Carry no purse, no bag, no sandals; and greet no one on the road.

"Whatever house you enter, first say, 'Peace to this house!' And if someone of peace is there, your peace will rest on that person; but if not, it will return to you. Remain in the same house, eating and drinking whatever they provide, for the labourer deserves his wage. Do not move about from house to house.

"Whenever you enter a town and its people welcome you, eat what is set before you; cure the sick who are there, and say to them, 'The kingdom of God has come near to you.'

* * *

"But whenever you enter a town and they do not welcome you, go out into its streets and say, 'Even the dust of your town that clings to our feet, we wipe off in protest against you. Yet know this: the kingdom of God has come near.' I tell you, on that day it will be more tolerable for Sodom than for that town."

The seventy returned with joy, saying, "Lord, in your name even the demons submit to us!" Jesus said to them, "I watched Satan fall from heaven like a flash of lightning. See, I have given you authority to tread on snakes and scorpions, and over all the power of the enemy; and nothing will hurt you.

"Nevertheless, do not rejoice at this, that the spirits submit to you, but rejoice that your names are written in heaven."

The Gospel of the Lord. **Praise to you, Lord Jesus Christ.**

Not only was Jerusalem the name of the capital city of Israel, but it also became a poetic name for all the chosen people of God.

When we hear the word "nurse," we usually think of someone who cares for the sick. Nursing is also how a mother feeds her infant, using milk from her own body. The Prophet Isaiah is trying to explain how great are God's love and care for his people, and so he chooses an image of the strongest and fiercest love he can imagine — the love of a mother for her child.

Awesome deeds are acts that inspire wonder and surprise; they are majestic and thrilling.

The Christians of Galatia began to get confused because some preachers were telling them that to be Christians, they first had to convert to Judaism and follow the entire Jewish law. Saint Paul wrote to the Galatians to reassure them and explain to them the importance of following Jesus' teachings.

When Saint Paul said that a new creation is more important than being circumcised, he was explaining that, for Christians, it is important to be united with Jesus through baptism and live the way he taught us to live.

The marks of Jesus that Saint Paul bears on his body are the physical signs of the sufferings he has endured — from flogging, illness and imprisonment. He also calls them "brands" — permanent marks on the skin to show that Paul proudly belongs to Christ.

In this story, the Lord of the harvest is God. We, the followers of Jesus, are workers in the fields: sowing the Word of God in order to bring people back to God. God wants more workers to help bring in the harvest.

July 14

15th Sunday in Ordinary Time

Moses spoke to the people, saying, "Obey the Lord your God by observing his commandments and decrees that are written in this book of the Law; turn to the Lord your God with all your heart and with all your soul.

"Surely this commandment that I am commanding you today is not too hard for you, nor is it too far away. It is not in heaven, that you should say, 'Who will go up to heaven for us, and get it for us so that we may hear it and observe it?'

"Neither is it beyond the sea, that you should say, 'Who will cross to the other side of the sea for us, and get it for us so that we may hear it and observe it?'

"No, the word is very near to you; it is in your mouth and in your heart for you to observe."

The word of the Lord. **Thanks be to God.**

An alternate psalm follows.

Psalm 69

R. **Seek God in your need, and let your hearts revive.**

As for me, my prayer is to you, O Lord.
At an acceptable time, O God,
in the abundance of your steadfast love, answer me.
With your steadfast help, rescue me.
Answer me, O Lord, for your steadfast love is good;
according to your abundant mercy, turn to me. R.

But I am lowly and in pain;
let your salvation, O God, protect me.
I will praise the name of God with a song;
I will magnify him with thanksgiving. R.

Let the oppressed see it and be glad;
you who seek God, let your hearts revive. R.

For God will save Zion
and rebuild the cities of Judah;
the children of his servants shall inherit it,
those who love his name shall live in it. R.

or

R. **The precepts of the Lord are right,**
and give joy to the heart.

The law of the Lord is perfect,
reviving the soul;
the decrees of the Lord are sure,
making wise the simple. R.

The precepts of the Lord are right,
rejoicing the heart;
the commandment of the Lord is clear,
enlightening the eyes. R.

The fear of the Lord is pure,
enduring forever;
the ordinances of the Lord are true
and righteous altogether. R.

More to be desired are they than gold,
even much fine gold;
sweeter also than honey,
and drippings of the honeycomb. R.

A reading from the Letter of Saint Paul to the Colossians (1.15-20)

Christ is the image of the invisible God, the firstborn of all creation; for in him all things in heaven and on earth were created, things visible and invisible, whether thrones or dominions or rulers or powers — all things have been created through him and for him.

Christ is before all things, and in him all things hold together. He is the head of the body, the Church; he is the beginning, the firstborn from the dead, so that he might come to have first place in everything.

For in Christ all the fullness of God was pleased to dwell, and through him God was pleased to reconcile to himself all things, whether on earth or in heaven, by making peace through the blood of his Cross.

The word of the Lord. **Thanks be to God.**

A lawyer stood up to test Jesus. "Teacher," he said, "what must I do to inherit eternal life?"

Jesus said to him, "What is written in the Law? What do you read there?" The lawyer answered, "You shall love the Lord your God with all your heart, and with all your soul, and with all your strength, and with all your mind; and your neighbour as yourself."

And Jesus said to him, "You have given the right answer; do this, and you will live." But wanting to justify himself, the lawyer asked Jesus, "And who is my neighbour?"

Jesus replied, "A man was going down from Jerusalem to Jericho, and fell into the hands of robbers, who stripped him, beat him, and went away, leaving him half dead. Now by chance a priest was going down that road; and when he saw him, he passed by on the other side. So likewise a Levite, when he came to the place and saw him, passed by on the other side.

"But a Samaritan while travelling came near him; and when he saw him, he was moved with pity. He went to him and bandaged his wounds, having poured oil and wine on them. Then he put him on his own animal, brought him to an inn, and took care of him.

"The next day the Samaritan took out two denarii, gave them to the innkeeper, and said, 'Take care of him; and when I come back, I will repay you whatever more you spend.'"

Jesus asked, "Which of these three, do you think, was a neighbour to the man who fell into the hands of the robbers?" The lawyer said, "The one who showed him mercy." Jesus said to him, "Go and do likewise."

The Gospel of the Lord. **Praise to you, Lord Jesus Christ.**

Deuteronomy is a book in the Old Testament or Hebrew Scriptures which teaches that there is only one God, and that the people of God should be united. Its name comes from the Greek word meaning "the second law" and refers to the second time that God gave the law to the people. It was written 600 years before Christ.

A commandment is an order given by God that must be followed. The Ten Commandments are rules to live by that were given by God to the people through Moses. To obey the Ten Commandments is to live as faithful children of God.

It is not enough to know God's commandments "in your head." Neither is it enough to learn them by memory so as to be able to recite them. God asks that you obey them gladly, that you hold them in your heart, as close as can be.

Jesus is the firstborn of all creation. Before he was born of the Virgin Mary — even before God created the world — he existed as the second person of the Trinity, the Son of God.

Thrones, dominations, rulers or powers are names for the multitudes of angels in heaven in all their different categories. As amazing as the angels are, they are created by God who is greater and more powerful than all he has created.

A lawyer is an expert on laws. Lawyers are trained to ask challenging questions as part of their work. The lawyer in today's Gospel is testing Jesus to see if he will make a mistake. But Jesus answers with truth and authority.

Levites had the responsibility to carry and care for the Ark of the Covenant while the Israelites wandered in the desert. From then on, they continued to be a priestly people.

In Jesus' time the Samaritans and the Judeans did not get along well. They differed on many religious questions and were forbidden to speak to each other. People hearing the parable of the Good Samaritan would have been astounded that a Samaritan would stop to help someone who was travelling from Jerusalem, the holy city of the Jews.

16th Sunday in Ordinary Time

A reading from the book of Genesis (18.1-10)

The Lord appeared to Abraham by the oaks of Mamre, as Abraham sat at the entrance of his tent in the heat of the day. Abraham looked up and saw three men standing near him. When he saw them, he ran from the tent entrance to meet them, and bowed down to the ground.

He said, "My lord, if I find favour with you, do not pass by your servant. Let a little water be brought, and wash your feet, and rest yourselves under the tree. Let me bring a little bread, that you may refresh yourselves, and after that you may pass on — since you have come to your servant." So they said, "Do as you have said."

And Abraham hastened into the tent to Sarah, and said, "Make ready quickly three measures of choice flour, knead it, and make cakes." Abraham ran to the herd, and took a calf, tender and good, and gave it to the servant, who hastened to prepare it. Then he took curds and milk and the calf that he had prepared, and set it before them; and he stood by them under the tree while they ate.

They said to Abraham, "Where is your wife Sarah?" And he said, "There, in the tent."

Then one said, "I will surely return to you in due season, and your wife Sarah shall have a son."

The word of the Lord. **Thanks be to God.**

Psalm 15

R. **O Lord, who may abide in your tent?**

Whoever walks blamelessly, and does what is right,
and speaks the truth from their heart;
whoever does not slander with their tongue. R.

Whoever does no evil to a friend,
nor takes up a reproach against a neighbour;
in whose eyes the wicked one is despised,
but who honours those who fear the Lord. R.

Whoever stands by their oath even to their hurt;
who does not lend money at interest,
and does not take a bribe against the innocent.
One who does these things shall never be moved. R.

A reading from the Letter of Saint Paul to the Colossians (1.24-28)

Brothers and sisters: I am now rejoicing in my sufferings for your sake, and in my flesh I am completing what is lacking in Christ's afflictions for the sake of his body, that is, the Church.

I became its servant according to God's commission that was given to me for you, to make the word of God fully known, the mystery that has been hidden throughout the ages and generations but has now been revealed to his saints.

To them God chose to make known how great among the Gentiles are the riches of the glory of this mystery, which is Christ in you, the hope of glory. It is Christ whom we proclaim, warning every person and teaching every person in all wisdom, so that we may present every person mature in Christ.

The word of the Lord. **Thanks be to God.**

A reading from the holy Gospel according to Luke (10.38-42)

Now as Jesus and his disciples went on their way, he entered a certain village, where a woman named Martha welcomed him into her home. She had a sister named Mary, who sat at the Lord's feet and listened to what he was saying.

But Martha was distracted by her many tasks; so she came to Jesus and asked, "Lord, do you not care that my sister has left me to do all the work by myself? Tell her then to help me."

But the Lord answered her, "Martha, Martha, you are worried and distracted by many things; there is need of only one thing. Mary has chosen the better part, which will not be taken away from her."

The Gospel of the Lord.
**Praise to you,
Lord Jesus Christ.**

Abraham was the first man to have faith in the one true God. God rewarded Abraham's faithfulness by giving him a son, Isaac, from whom the people of Israel descended. Because Abraham is the father of the Hebrew people, he is the father of Judaism, Christianity and Islam.

A psalm is a prayer that is sung. In the Bible the book of Psalms has 150 prayers that reflect the way the people of Israel prayed. The psalms continue to teach us how to pray. In the Mass, after the first reading, a psalm is sung or said.

Saint Paul wrote a letter to the Colossians, members of a Christian community in the town of Colossae (in what is now Turkey). They were doubting their faith, but Paul's letter reminded them that Christ is above and before everything.

Saint Paul saw his own afflictions or suffering as part of the sufferings of Christ. Paul's hardships united him in a special way to Jesus, so that even though his life was hard, he found joy in his closeness to Jesus.

The mystery of God that Saint Paul mentions is God's plan for all humanity to be redeemed by his Son and live as children of God. This plan was revealed slowly by the prophets, until Jesus revealed it completely by his death and resurrection.

When Jesus says that Mary has chosen the better part over her sister Martha, he is letting us know that to be Jesus' friend — to listen to his word — is the most important thing to do. Martha would have done better to put her work aside for a while and honour Jesus with her presence and attention.

July 28

17th Sunday in Ordinary Time

The Lord said: "How great is the outcry against Sodom and Gomorrah and how very grave their sin! I must go down and see whether they have done altogether according to the outcry that has come to me; and if not, I will know."

So the men turned from there, and went toward Sodom, while Abraham remained standing before the Lord. Then Abraham came near and said, "Will you indeed sweep away the righteous with the wicked? Suppose there are fifty righteous within the city; will you then sweep away the place and not forgive it for the fifty righteous who are in it? Far be it from you to do such a thing, to slay the righteous with the wicked, so that the righteous fare as the wicked! Far be that from you! Shall not the Judge of all the earth do what is just?" And the Lord said, "If I find at Sodom fifty righteous in the city, I will forgive the whole place for their sake."

Abraham answered, "Let me take it upon myself to speak to the Lord, I who am but dust and ashes. Suppose five of the fifty righteous are lacking? Will you destroy the whole city for lack of five?" And the Lord said, "I will not destroy it if I find forty-five there."

Again Abraham spoke to the Lord, "Suppose forty are found there." He answered, "For the sake of forty I will not do it."

Then Abraham said, "Oh do not let the Lord be angry if I speak. Suppose thirty are found there." The Lord answered, "I will not do it, if I find thirty there."

Abraham said, "Let me take it upon myself to speak to the Lord. Suppose twenty are found there." The Lord answered, "For the sake of twenty I will not destroy it."

Then Abraham said, "Oh do not let the Lord be angry if I speak just once more. Suppose ten are found there." The Lord answered, "For the sake of ten I will not destroy it."

The word of the Lord. **Thanks be to God.**

R. **On the day I called, O Lord, you answered me.**

I give you thanks, O Lord, with my whole heart;
before the Angels I sing your praise;
I bow down toward your holy temple,
and give thanks to your name
for your steadfast love and your faithfulness. R.

For you have exalted your name
and your word above everything.
On the day I called, you answered me,
you increased my strength of soul. R.

For though the Lord is high, he regards the lowly;
but the haughty he perceives from far away.
Though I walk in the midst of trouble,
you preserve me against the wrath of my enemies. R.

You stretch out your hand and your right hand delivers me.
The Lord will fulfill his purpose for me;
your steadfast love, O Lord, endures forever.
Do not forsake the work of your hands. R.

A reading from the Letter of Saint Paul to the Colossians (2.12-14)

Brothers and sisters, When you were buried with Christ in baptism, you were also raised with him through faith in the power of God, who raised Christ from the dead.

And when you were dead in trespasses and the uncircumcision of your flesh, God made you alive together with him, when he forgave us all our trespasses, erasing the record that stood against us with its legal demands. He set this aside, nailing it to the Cross.

The word of the Lord. **Thanks be to God.**

Jesus was praying in a certain place, and after he had finished, one of his disciples said to him, "Lord, teach us to pray, as John taught his disciples."

He said to them, "When you pray, say: 'Father, hallowed be your name. Your kingdom come. Give us each day our daily bread. And forgive us our sins, for we ourselves forgive everyone indebted to us. And lead us not into temptation.'"

And Jesus said to the disciples, "Suppose one of you has a friend, and you go to him at midnight and say to him, 'Friend, lend me three loaves of bread; for a friend of mine has arrived, and I have nothing to set before him.' And your friend answers from within, 'Do not bother me; the door has already been locked, and my children are with me in bed; I cannot get up and give you anything.'

"I tell you, even though he will not get up and give him anything because he is his friend, at least because of his persistence he will get up and give him whatever he needs.

"So I say to you: Ask, and it will be given you; search, and you will find; knock, and the door will be opened for you. For everyone who asks receives, and everyone who searches finds, and for everyone who knocks, the door will be opened.

"Is there any father among you who, if your child asks for a fish, will give the child a snake instead of a fish? Or if the child asks for an egg, will give a scorpion?

"If you then, who are evil, know how to give good gifts to your children, how much more will the heavenly Father give the Holy Spirit to those who ask him!"

The Gospel of the Lord. **Praise to you, Lord Jesus Christ.**

The two cities of Sodom and Gomorrah had disappeared by Jesus' time, but their story in the book of Genesis was well known. They were mentioned as symbols of evil; there were no worse cities.

When Abraham calls himself dust and ashes, he expresses how small he feels before God. It is a way of saying that he is worth very little — too worthless to make a petition to God. The dust also reminds us that God created human beings from dust.

To be dead in trespasses is to be burdened by the weight of our sins. When we are united to Jesus through baptism and ask for God's forgiveness for our sins, we find new life in Jesus.

Jesus was frequently found praying, especially during the most important moments of his life. It is very important for all of us to learn to quiet our hearts in order to speak and listen to God.

In the Our Father, when we say "hallowed be thy name," we are declaring that God's name should be made holy or hallowed. It is a way of saying, "Blessed be you" — your holiness and grandeur will be known everywhere.

Jesus said, "Ask, and it will be given you." This teaches us to have every confidence that God listens to us and will always give us what we most need in order to live as God's children.

August 4

18th Sunday in Ordinary Time

A reading from the book of Ecclesiastes (1.2; 2.21-23)

Vanity of vanities, says the Teacher,
vanity of vanities! All is vanity.

Sometimes one who has toiled
with wisdom and knowledge and skill
must leave all to be enjoyed by another
who did not toil for it.
This also is vanity and a great evil.

What does a person get from all their toil and strain,
their toil under the sun?
For their days are full of pain,
and their work is a vexation;
even at night their mind does not rest.
This also is vanity.

The word of the Lord. **Thanks be to God.**

Psalm 90

R. **Lord, you have been our dwelling place in all generations.**

You turn man back to dust, and say,
"Turn back, you children of Adam."
For a thousand years in your sight
are like yesterday when it is past,
or like a watch in the night. R.

You sweep them away; they are like a dream,
like grass that is renewed in the morning;
in the morning it flourishes and is renewed;
in the evening it fades and withers. R.

So teach us to count our days
that we may gain a wise heart.
Turn, O Lord! How long?
Have compassion on your servants! R.

Satisfy us in the morning with your steadfast love,
so that we may rejoice and be glad all our days.
Let the favour of the Lord our God be upon us,
and prosper for us the work of our hands. R.

A reading from the Letter of Saint Paul to the Colossians (3.1-5, 9-11)

Brothers and sisters: If you have been raised with Christ, seek the things that are above, where Christ is, seated at the right hand of God.

Set your minds on things that are above, not on things that are on earth, for you have died, and your life is hidden with Christ in God. When Christ who is your life is revealed, then you also will be revealed with him in glory.

Put to death, therefore, whatever in you is earthly: fornication, impurity, passion, evil desire, and greed, which is idolatry.

Do not lie to one another, seeing that you have stripped off the old self with its practices and have clothed yourselves with the new self, which is being renewed in knowledge according to the image of its creator.

In that renewal there is no longer Greek and Jew, circumcised and uncircumcised, barbarian, Scythian, slave and free; but Christ is all and in all!

The word of the Lord. **Thanks be to God.**

A reading from the holy Gospel according to Luke (12.13-21)

Someone in the crowd said to Jesus, "Teacher, tell my brother to divide the family inheritance with me." But Jesus said to him, "Friend, who set me to be a judge or arbitrator over you?"

And Jesus said to the crowd, "Take care! Be on your guard against all kinds of greed; for one's life does not consist in the abundance of possessions."

Then Jesus told them a parable: "The land of a rich man produced abundantly. And he thought to himself, 'What should I do, for I have no place to store my crops?' Then he said, 'I will do this: I will pull down my barns and build larger ones, and there I will store all my grain and my goods. And I will say to my soul, "Soul, you have ample goods laid up for many years; relax, eat, drink, be merry."'

"But God said to him, 'You fool! This very night your life is being demanded of you. And the things you have prepared, whose will they be?' So it is with those who store up treasures for themselves but are not rich toward God."

The Gospel of the Lord. **Praise to you, Lord Jesus Christ.**

221

Ecclesiastes is a book in the Old Testament written 300 years before Christ. Its message is not to worry about every little thing, but to take pleasure in God's gifts and to keep God's commandments.

When Saint Paul mentions the things that are above, he is referring to all that helps us live as children of God, following the teachings of Jesus. The things that are of earth are those things that fill us with worry or lead us away from Jesus.

As Christians we are all called to be revealed with him in glory — to live our life in such a way that it is clear we are close to Jesus. When Jesus comes again, all who have died will be gathered to him in glory.

Greed is an urge in our hearts for more things, more money, more clothes, more toys... even though we don't need them. When we are ruled by greed, we forget that there are people more in need than ourselves.

We are rich toward God when we reject greed and live as brothers and sisters — helping those who are in need, the sick, the poor, the lonely. Our wealth is measured not by our worldly possessions but by how we have lived our life.

19th Sunday in Ordinary Time

A reading from the book of Wisdom (18.6-9)

The night of the deliverance from Egypt was made known beforehand to our ancestors, so that they might rejoice in sure knowledge of the oaths in which they trusted.

The deliverance of the righteous and the destruction of their enemies were expected by your people. For by the same means by which you punished our enemies you called us to yourself and glorified us.

For in secret the holy children of good people offered sacrifices, and with one accord agreed to the divine law, so that the saints would share alike the same things, both blessings and dangers; and already they were singing the praises of the ancestors.

The word of the Lord. **Thanks be to God.**

Psalm 33

R. **Blessed the people the Lord has chosen as his heritage.**

Rejoice in the Lord, O you righteous.
Praise befits the upright.
Blessed is the nation whose God is the Lord,
the people whom he has chosen as his heritage. R.

Truly the eye of the Lord is on those who fear him,
on those who hope in his steadfast love,
to deliver their soul from death,
and to keep them alive in famine. R.

Our soul waits for the Lord;
he is our help and shield.
Let your steadfast love, O Lord, be upon us,
even as we hope in you. R.

The shorter version ends at the asterisks.

Brothers and sisters: Faith is the assurance of things hoped for, the conviction of things not seen. Indeed, by faith our ancestors received approval.

By faith Abraham obeyed when he was called to set out for a place that he was to receive as an inheritance; and he set out, not knowing where he was going. By faith he stayed for a time in the land he had been promised, as in a foreign land, living in tents, as did Isaac and Jacob, who were heirs with him of the same promise.

For Abraham looked forward to the city that has foundations, whose architect and builder is God. By faith Sarah herself, though barren, received power to conceive, even when she was too old, because she considered him faithful who had promised.

Therefore from one person, and this one as good as dead, descendants were born, "as many as the stars of heaven and as the innumerable grains of sand by the seashore."

* * *

All of these died in faith without having received the promises, but from a distance they saw and greeted them. They confessed that they were strangers and foreigners on the earth, for people who speak in this way make it clear that they are seeking a homeland. If they had been thinking of the land that they had left behind, they would have had opportunity to return.

But as it is, they desire a better country, that is, a heavenly one. Therefore God is not ashamed to be called their God; indeed, he has prepared a city for them.

By faith Abraham, when put to the test, offered up Isaac. He who had received the promises was ready to offer up his only-begotten son, of whom he had been told, "It is through Isaac that descendants shall be named for you." Abraham considered the fact that God is able even to raise someone from the dead — and figuratively speaking, he did receive Isaac back.

The word of the Lord. **Thanks be to God.**

For the shorter version, omit the indented parts.

Jesus said to his disciples, "Do not be afraid, little flock, for it is your Father's good pleasure to give you the kingdom. Sell your possessions, and give alms. Make purses for yourselves that do not wear out, an unfailing treasure in heaven, where no thief comes near and no moth destroys. For where your treasure is, there your heart will be also.

"Be dressed for action and have your lamps lit; be like those who are waiting for their master to return from the wedding banquet, so that they may open the door for him as soon as he comes and knocks. Blessed are those slaves whom the master finds alert when he comes; truly I tell you, he will fasten his belt and have them sit down to eat, and he will come and serve them. If he comes during the middle of the night, or near dawn, and finds them so, blessed are those slaves.

"But know this: if the owner of the house had known at what hour the thief was coming, he would not have let his house be broken into. You also must be ready, for the Son of Man is coming at an unexpected hour."

Peter said, "Lord, are you telling this parable for us or for everyone?" And the Lord said, "Who then is the faithful and prudent manager whom his master will put in charge of his slaves, to give them their allowance of food at the proper time? Blessed is that slave whom his master will find at work when he arrives. Truly I tell you, he will put that one in charge of all his possessions. But if that slave says to himself, 'My master is delayed in coming,' and if he begins to beat the other slaves, men and women, and to eat and drink and get drunk, the master of that slave will come on a day when he does not expect him and at an hour that he does not know, and will cut him in pieces, and put him with the unfaithful.

"That slave who knew what his master wanted, but did not prepare himself or do what was wanted, will receive a severe beating. But the one who did not know and did what deserved a beating will receive a light beating. From everyone to whom much has been given, much will be required; and from the one to whom much has been entrusted, even more will be demanded."

The Gospel of the Lord. **Praise to you, Lord Jesus Christ.**

The book of Wisdom is part of the Old Testament written shortly before Jesus was born. It teaches that the truly wise person lives a faithful life and strives for justice.

The letter to the Hebrews is found in the New Testament. Its author is unknown. More than a letter, it appears to be a very solemn sermon. It encourages us to remember that Jesus Christ is our merciful priest who offered his life as a sacrifice on our behalf.

Isaac, the son of Abraham and Sarah, inherited the promise made to Abraham that he would father a great family who would become the chosen people of God. Jacob was the son of Isaac and Rebecca who astutely won this promised inheritance from his twin brother Esau. Jacob had twelve sons who founded the twelve tribes of Israel.

A wedding banquet is a reception held after two people get married. The Bible often refers to the arrival of the reign of God as such a feast where all people will be welcome. It will be a time of great joy and celebration.

In the Gospels Jesus calls himself the Son of Man. Jesus uses this title to show he is a human being, and tells his disciples that although he will suffer greatly, his suffering will not overcome him.

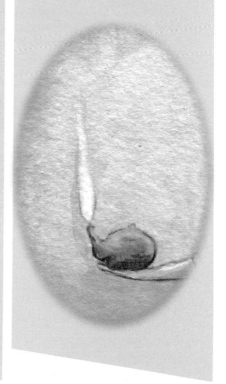

20th Sunday In Ordinary Time

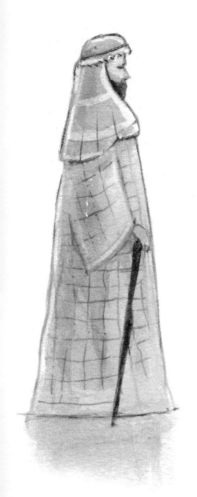

The officials said to the king, "This man ought to be put to death, because he is discouraging the soldiers who are left in this city, and all the people, by speaking such words to them. For this man is not seeking the welfare of this people, but their harm."

King Zedekiah said, "Here he is; he is in your hands; for the king is powerless against you."

So they took Jeremiah and threw him into the cistern of Malchiah, the king's son, which was in the court of the guard, letting Jeremiah down by ropes. Now there was no water in the cistern, but only mud, and Jeremiah sank in the mud.

So Ebed-melech the Ethiopian, an officer in the king's house, left the king's house and spoke to the king, "My lord king, these men have acted wickedly in all they did to the Prophet Jeremiah by throwing him into the cistern to die there of hunger, for there is no bread left in the city." Then the king commanded Ebed-melech the Ethiopian, "Take three men with you from here, and pull the Prophet Jeremiah up from the cistern before he dies."

The word of the Lord. **Thanks be to God.**

Psalm 40

R. **Lord, make haste to help me!**

I waited patiently for the Lord;
he inclined to me and heard my cry. R.

He drew me up from the desolate pit,
out of the miry bog,
and set my feet upon a rock,
making my steps secure. R.

He put a new song in my mouth,
a song of praise to our God.
Many will see and fear,
and put their trust in the Lord. R.

As for me, I am poor and needy,
but the Lord takes thought for me.
You are my help and my deliverer;
do not delay, O my God. R.

A reading from the Letter to the Hebrews (12.1-4)

Brothers and sisters: Since we are surrounded by so great a cloud of witnesses, let us also lay aside every weight and the sin that clings so closely, and let us run with perseverance the race that is set before us, looking to Jesus the pioneer and perfecter of our faith, who for the sake of the joy that was set before him endured the Cross, disregarding its shame, and has taken his seat at the right hand of the throne of God.

Consider Jesus who endured such hostility against himself from sinners, so that you may not grow weary or lose heart. In your struggle against sin you have not yet resisted to the point of shedding your blood.

The word of the Lord. **Thanks be to God.**

A reading from the holy Gospel according to Luke (12.49-53)

Jesus said to his disciples: "I came to bring fire to the earth, and how I wish it were already kindled! I have a baptism with which to be baptized, and what stress I am under until it is completed!

"Do you think that I have come to bring peace to the earth? No, I tell you, but rather division! From now on five in one household will be divided, three against two and two against three; they will be divided: father against son and son against father, mother against daughter and daughter against mother, mother-in-law against her daughter-in-law and daughter-in-law against mother-in-law."

The Gospel of the Lord. **Praise to you, Lord Jesus Christ.**

Zedekiah was king of Israel at the time of the prophet Jeremiah. Jeremiah was the king's counsellor, but the king did not treat him well.

A cistern is a deep structure, like a well, where water is collected for future use. Cisterns are commonly found in areas with little rainfall. Because they are so deep, they are dangerous, whether wet or dry.

A miry bog is an impassable swamp. This psalm echoes the story of Jeremiah that we have just heard, where Jeremiah is thrown into a cistern with a deep, muddy bottom.

The cloud of witnesses surrounding us are the saints and good Christians who came before us and showed us by their example how to live the faith. We are strengthened and supported by this great communion of saints.

Although many holy priests and prophets came before Jesus, he was the perfecter of our faith, because he explained the writings and fulfilled the prophecies through his life, death and resurrection.

To bring peace is to bring tranquillity and the absence of strife to a situation. Jesus is telling us that we must make radical changes to our lives in order to follow him. Following the path of Jesus leads through death to new life.

August 25

21st Sunday in Ordinary Time

Thus says the Lord: "For I know their works and their thoughts, and I am coming to gather all nations and tongues; and they shall come and shall see my glory, and I will set a sign among them.

"From them I will send survivors to the nations, to Tarshish, Put, and Lud — which draw the bow — to Tubal and Javan, to the coastlands far away that have not heard of my fame or seen my glory; and they shall declare my glory among the nations.

"They shall bring all your kindred from all the nations as an offering to the Lord, on horses, and in chariots, and in litters, and on mules, and on dromedaries, to my holy mountain Jerusalem," says the Lord, "just as the children of Israel bring a grain offering in a clean vessel to the house of the Lord.

"And I will also take some of them as priests and as Levites," says the Lord.

The word of the Lord. **Thanks be to God.**

Psalm 117

R̰ **Go into all the world and proclaim the good news.**

or **Alleluia!**

Praise the Lord, all you nations!
Extol him, all you peoples! R̰

For great is his steadfast love toward us,
and the faithfulness of the Lord endures forever. R̰

A reading from the Letter to the Hebrews (12.5-7, 11-13)

Brothers and sisters: You have forgotten the exhortation that addresses you as children — "My son, do not regard lightly the discipline of the Lord, or lose heart when you are punished by him; for the Lord disciplines the one whom he loves, and chastises every son whom he accepts."

Endure trials for the sake of discipline. God is treating you as sons; for what son is there whom a father does not discipline?

Now, discipline always seems painful rather than pleasant at the time, but later it yields the peaceful fruit of righteousness to those who have been trained by it.

Therefore lift your drooping hands and strengthen your weak knees, and make straight paths for your feet, so that what is lame may not be put out of joint, but rather be healed.

The word of the Lord. **Thanks be to God.**

A reading from the holy Gospel according to Luke (13.22-30)

Jesus went through one town and village after another, teaching as he made his way to Jerusalem. Someone asked him, "Lord, will only a few be saved?"

Jesus said to them, "Strive to enter through the narrow door; for many, I tell you, will try to enter and will not be able.

"When once the owner of the house has got up and shut the door, and you begin to stand outside and to knock at the door, saying, 'Lord, open to us,' then in reply he will say to you, 'I do not know where you come from.'

"Then you will begin to say, 'We ate and drank with you, and you taught in our streets.' But the Lord will say, 'I do not know where you come from; go away from me, all you evildoers!'

"There will be weeping and gnashing of teeth when you see Abraham and Isaac and Jacob and all the Prophets in the kingdom of God, and you yourselves thrown out. Then people will come from east and west, from north and south, and will eat in the kingdom of God. Indeed, some are last who will be first, and some are first who will be last."

The Gospel of the Lord. **Praise to you, Lord Jesus Christ.**

To see the glory of God means to recognize God's importance, power and authority. It is to accept the true God.

The moment when all the people in the world arrive in Jerusalem, the city of peace, is the moment when all humanity will be united in faith to their Creator, who led the people of Israel out of slavery in Egypt.

The letter to the Hebrews teaches us to see discipline or correction from God as an opportunity to grow. God can use even our sufferings to help us live better lives and grow in love.

The Gospel of Saint Luke was written for Christians who were not Jewish. It is also known as the Gospel of mercy. The Acts of the Apostles was also written by Saint Luke.

To enter a room by a narrow door is not an easy thing to do: it takes some effort. Jesus uses this image in order to tell us to be persistent in doing good and loving our neighbour. This way our friendship with Jesus will grow and we will enter the kingdom of heaven.

When Jesus speaks of the kingdom of God, he means the end of time when God's reign will be complete and when all people will live in unity and peace.

22nd Sunday in Ordinary Time

A reading from the book of Sirach (3.17-20, 28-29)

My child, perform your tasks with humility; then you will be loved by those whom God accepts. The greater you are, the more you must humble yourself; so you will find favour in the sight of the Lord. Many are lofty and renowned, but to the humble the Lord reveals his secrets. For great is the might of the Lord; but by the humble he is glorified.

When calamity befalls someone proud, there is no healing, for an evil plant has taken root in them.

The mind of the intelligent appreciates proverbs, and an attentive ear is the desire of the wise.

The word of the Lord. **Thanks be to God.**

Psalm 68

R. **In your goodness, O God, you provided for the needy.**

Let the righteous be joyful;
let them exult before God;
let them be jubilant with joy.
Sing to God, sing praises to his name;
his name is the Lord,
be exultant before him. R.

Father of orphans and protector of widows
is God in his holy habitation.
God gives the desolate a home to live in;
he leads out the prisoners to prosperity. R.

Rain in abundance, O God,
you showered abroad;
you restored your heritage when it languished;
your flock found a dwelling in it;
in your goodness, O God,
you provided for the needy. R.

A reading from the Letter to the Hebrews
(12.18-19, 22-24)

Brothers and sisters: You have not come to something that can be touched, a blazing fire, and darkness, and gloom, and a tempest, and the sound of a trumpet, and a voice whose words made the hearers beg that not another word be spoken to them.

But you have come to Mount Zion and to the city of the living God, the heavenly Jerusalem, and to innumerable Angels in festal gathering, and to the assembly of the firstborn who are enrolled in heaven, and to God the judge of all, and to the spirits of the righteous made perfect, and to Jesus, the mediator of a new covenant.

The word of the Lord. **Thanks be to God.**

A reading from the holy Gospel according to Luke
(14.1, 7-14)

On one occasion when Jesus was going to the house of a leader of the Pharisees to eat a meal on the Sabbath, the lawyers and Pharisees were watching him closely. When Jesus noticed how the guests chose the places of honour, he told them a parable.

"When you are invited by someone to a wedding banquet, do not sit down at the place of honour, in case someone more distinguished than you has been invited by your host; and the host who invited both of you may come and say to you, 'Give this person your place,' and then in disgrace you would start to take the lowest place.

"But when you are invited, go and sit down at the lowest place, so that when your host comes, he may say to you, 'Friend, move up higher'; then you will be honoured in the presence of all who sit at the table with you. For whoever exalts himself will be humbled, and whoever humbles himself will be exalted."

Jesus said also to the Pharisee who had invited him, "When you give a luncheon or a dinner, do not invite your friends or your brothers or sisters or your relatives or rich neighbours, in case they may invite you in return, and you would be repaid. But when you give a banquet, invite the poor, the crippled, the lame, and the blind. And you will be blessed, because they cannot repay you, for you will be repaid at the resurrection of the righteous."

The Gospel of the Lord. **Praise to you, Lord Jesus Christ.**

The book of Sirach was written 200 years before Jesus was born. It deals with many topics, but especially with the nature of true wisdom: respect for God and obedience to God's plans for us.

When we have true humility, we learn to value ourselves as children of God. We do not feel overly important but we also do not undervalue the wonderful qualities that God gave to each of us.

A proud person is somebody who thinks they are better than others, and so puts other people down. We can be proud of our accomplishments, but not at the expense of other people.

Mount Zion was another name for the city of Jerusalem, which was very close to this rocky peak. Sometimes the great temple in Jerusalem was also referred to by this name.

One way to speak of the time when God will meet all those who have died in Christ is to refer to the heavenly Jerusalem.

The Pharisees were Jews who belonged to a very strict sect, one which followed all the religious rules but sometimes forgot to live with love. They were not well liked among the common people.

According to Jesus, it is most important to learn how to be generous, for true generosity expects nothing in return. Jesus challenges his host, the Pharisee who invited him to dinner, next time to invite the poor who have no hope of repaying the favour. The invitation is then a pure gift, given in generous love.

23rd Sunday in Ordinary Time

A reading from the book of Wisdom (9.13-18)

For who can learn the counsel of God?
Or who can discern what the Lord wills?
For the reasoning of mortals is worthless,
and our designs are likely to fail;
for a perishable body weighs down the soul,
and this earthly tent burdens the thoughtful mind.

We can hardly guess at what is on earth,
and what is at hand we find with labour;
but who has traced out what is in the heavens?
Who has learned your counsel,
unless you have given wisdom
and sent your holy spirit from on high?

And thus the paths of those on earth were set right,
and people were taught what pleases you,
and were saved by wisdom.

The word of the Lord. **Thanks be to God.**

Psalm 90

R̰ **Lord, you have been our dwelling place in all generations.**

You turn man back to dust, and say,
"Turn back, you children of Adam."
For a thousand years in your sight
are like yesterday when it is past,
or like a watch in the night. R̰

You sweep them away; they are like a dream,
like grass that is renewed in the morning;
in the morning it flourishes and is renewed;
in the evening it fades and withers. R̰

So teach us to count our days
that we may gain a wise heart.
Turn, O Lord! How long?
Have compassion on your servants! R̰

Satisfy us in the morning with your steadfast love,
so that we may rejoice and be glad all our days.
Let the favour of the Lord our God be upon us,
and prosper for us the work of our hands. R̰

A reading from the Letter of Saint Paul to Philemon
(9-10, 12-17)

Beloved: I, Paul, do this as an old man, and now also as a prisoner of Christ Jesus. I am appealing to you for my child, Onesimus, whose father I have become during my imprisonment.

I am sending him, that is, my own heart, back to you. I wanted to keep him with me, so that he might be of service to me in your place during my imprisonment for the Gospel; but I preferred to do nothing without your consent, in order that your good deed might be voluntary and not something forced.

Perhaps this is the reason he was separated from you for a while, so that you might have him back forever, no longer as a slave but more than a slave, a beloved brother — especially to me but how much more to you, both in the flesh and in the Lord.

So if you consider me your partner, welcome him as you would welcome me.

The word of the Lord. **Thanks be to God.**

A reading from the holy Gospel according to Luke
(14.25-33)

Large crowds were travelling with Jesus; and he turned and said to them, "Whoever comes to me and does not hate their father and mother, spouse and children, brothers and sisters, yes, and even their life itself, cannot be my disciple. Whoever does not carry their cross and follow me cannot be my disciple.

"For which of you, intending to build a tower, does not first sit down and estimate the cost, to see whether he has enough to complete it? Otherwise, when he has laid a foundation and is not able to finish, all who see it will begin to ridicule him, saying, 'This fellow began to build and was not able to finish.'

"Or what king, going out to wage war against another king, will not sit down first and consider whether he is able with ten thousand to oppose the one who comes against him with twenty thousand? If he cannot, then, while the other is still far away, he sends a delegation and asks for the terms of peace.

"So therefore, whoever of you does not give up all their possessions cannot be my disciple."

The Gospel of the Lord. **Praise to you, Lord Jesus Christ.**

The counsel or wisdom of God is God's plan for us, for all people and all creation. We cannot know the mind of God, but we can learn from the wisdom of the Prophets and the Church.

Wisdom is not something that comes by studying hard. Wisdom comes from prayer and lived experience; it is a gift of the Holy Spirit that helps us to make good decisions.

The letter written by Saint Paul to Philemon is a short but beautiful letter. It teaches that, for Christians, all men and women are equal: there should be no difference between Jews and Gentiles, between slaves and free people, because we are all brothers and sisters as children of God.

Saint Paul wrote to Philemon about having baptized Onesimus in jail, "whose father I have become" for Christ. Through baptism, Paul gave his friend life in the Spirit of God, and in this sense became his "spiritual father."

To follow Jesus means to decide to live as he lived, loving God above all else. Someone "comes to me," God says, if they follow Jesus and live justly, treating all people as their brothers and sisters.

A person "cannot be my disciple," Jesus says, if they are unable to give up everything else, even the best things in life. We have to be ready to leave our most cherished possessions, if necessary.

24th Sunday in Ordinary Time

The Lord said to Moses, "Go down at once! Your people, whom you brought up out of the land of Egypt, have acted perversely; they have been quick to turn aside from the way that I commanded them; they have cast for themselves an image of a calf, and have worshipped it and sacrificed to it, and said, 'These are your gods, O Israel, who brought you up out of the land of Egypt!'"

The Lord said to Moses, "I have seen this people, how stiff-necked they are. Now let me alone, so that my wrath may burn hot against them and I may consume them; and of you I will make a great nation."

But Moses implored the Lord his God, and said, "O Lord, why does your wrath burn hot against your people, whom you brought out of the land of Egypt with great power and with a mighty hand? Remember Abraham, Isaac, and Israel, your servants, how you swore to them by your own self, saying to them, 'I will multiply your descendants like the stars of heaven, and all this land that I have promised I will give to your descendants, and they shall inherit it forever.'"

And the Lord changed his mind about the disaster that he planned to bring on his people.

The word of the Lord. **Thanks be to God.**

R̥ **I will get up and go to my Father.**

Have mercy on me, O God,
according to your steadfast love;
according to your abundant mercy
blot out my transgressions.
Wash me thoroughly from my iniquity,
and cleanse me from my sin. R̥

Create in me a clean heart, O God,
and put a new and right spirit within me.
Do not cast me away from your presence,
and do not take your holy spirit from me. R̥

O Lord, open my lips,
and my mouth will declare your praise.
The sacrifice acceptable to God
is a broken spirit;
a broken and contrite heart, O God,
you will not despise. R̥

A reading from the first Letter of Saint Paul to Timothy (1.12-17)

Beloved: I am grateful to Christ Jesus our Lord, who has strengthened me, because he judged me faithful and appointed me to his service, even though I was formerly a blasphemer, a persecutor, and a man of violence.

But I received mercy because I had acted ignorantly in unbelief, and the grace of our Lord overflowed for me with the faith and love that are in Christ Jesus.

The saying is sure and worthy of full acceptance, that Christ Jesus came into the world to save sinners — of whom I am the foremost.

But for that very reason I received mercy, so that in me, as the foremost, Jesus Christ might display the utmost patience, making me an example to those who would come to believe in him for eternal life.

To the King of the ages, immortal, invisible, the only God, be honour and glory forever and ever. Amen.

The word of the Lord. **Thanks be to God.**

The shorter version ends at the asterisks.

All the tax collectors and sinners were coming near to listen to Jesus. And the Pharisees and the scribes were grumbling and saying, "This fellow welcomes sinners and eats with them."

So he told them a parable: "Which one of you, having a hundred sheep and losing one of them, does not leave the ninety-nine in the wilderness and go after the one that is lost until he finds it? When he has found it, he lays it on his shoulders and rejoices. And when he comes home, he calls together his friends and neighbours, saying to them, 'Rejoice with me, for I have found my sheep that was lost.' Just so, I tell you, there will be more joy in heaven over one sinner who repents than over ninety-nine righteous persons who need no repentance.

"Or what woman having ten silver coins, if she loses one of them, does not light a lamp, sweep the house, and search carefully until she finds it? When she has found it, she calls together her friends and neighbours, saying, 'Rejoice with me, for I have found the coin that I had lost.' Just so, I tell you, there is joy in the presence of the Angels of God over one sinner who repents."

* * *

Then Jesus said, "There was a man who had two sons. The younger of them said to his father, 'Father, give me the share of the property that will belong to me.' So the father divided his property between them.

"A few days later the younger son gathered all he had and travelled to a distant country, and there he squandered his property in dissolute living. When he had spent everything, a severe famine took place throughout that country, and he began

247

to be in need. So he went and hired himself out to one of the citizens of that country, who sent him to his fields to feed the pigs. The young man would gladly have filled himself with the pods that the pigs were eating; and no one gave him anything.

"But when he came to himself he said, 'How many of my father's hired hands have bread enough and to spare, but here I am dying of hunger! I will get up and go to my father, and I will say to him, "Father, I have sinned against heaven and before you; I am no longer worthy to be called your son; treat me like one of your hired hands."'

"So he set off and went to his father. But while he was still far off, his father saw him and was filled with compassion; he ran and put his arms around him and kissed him. Then the son said to him, 'Father, I have sinned against heaven and before you; I am no longer worthy to be called your son.'

"But the father said to his slaves, 'Quickly, bring out a robe — the best one — and put it on him; put a ring on his finger and sandals on his feet. And get the fatted calf and kill it, and let us eat and celebrate; for this son of mine was dead and is alive again; he was lost and is found!' And they began to celebrate.

"Now his elder son was in the field; and when he came and approached the house, he heard music and dancing. He called one of the slaves and asked what was going on. The slave replied, 'Your brother has come, and your father has killed the fatted calf, because he has got him back safe and sound.'

"Then the elder son became angry and refused to go in. His father came out and began to plead with him. But he answered his father, 'Listen! For all these years I have been working like a slave for you, and I have never disobeyed your command; yet you have never given me even a young goat so that I might celebrate with my friends. But when this son of yours came back, who has devoured your property with prostitutes, you killed the fatted calf for him!'

"Then the father said to him, 'Son, you are always with me, and all that is mine is yours. But we had to celebrate and rejoice, because this brother of yours was dead and has come to life; he was lost and has been found.'"

The Gospel of the Lord. **Praise to you, Lord Jesus Christ.**

The second book in the Bible is called Exodus, which means "exit" or "migration." It tells the story of how God liberated the Israelites from slavery in Egypt. Moses was the people's guide and the person who, as God's messenger, gave them the Ten Commandments.

Someone who has acted perversely is someone who once was good, but who then very deliberately behaved badly. After they were freed from slavery in Egypt, the Israelites soon forgot God's goodness and returned to their old ways.

Egypt was the land of the Pharaohs where the Hebrew people went to live when their own land was suffering a severe famine. Over time, the Egyptians made the Hebrews their slaves. For this reason, when the Bible mentioned Egypt, the people understood the reference to slavery and how God liberated them.

Timothy was a companion of Saint Paul. He helped Paul to spread the Gospel and was thrown into jail with his master. In the New Testament there are two letters to Timothy, where Saint Paul gives him advice as the person responsible for the Church in Ephesus.

In the early Church, Christians began to refer to the resurrected Jesus as Christ Jesus. This title connects two names: Christ which means "the anointed one," and Jesus ("God saves") which was the name the angel told Mary and Joseph to give their child.

The tax collectors were local men who worked for the Romans, and therefore were seen as traitors and despised by the Jews. Many tax collectors were also cheats, taking more money than was their due.

The scribes were people who knew the law very well. To their way of thinking, it was most important to observe the law. Their idea of God was a fearful one, because God was seen as someone who might punish them if they broke the rules.

25th Sunday in Ordinary Time

OLIVE OIL
-100 Jugs
GRAIN -100

Hear this, you that trample on the needy, and bring to ruin the poor of the land, saying, "When will the new moon be over so that we may sell grain; and the Sabbath, so that we may offer wheat for sale? We will measure out less and charge more, and tamper with the scales, buying the poor for silver and the needy for a pair of sandals, and selling the sweepings of the wheat."

The Lord has sworn by the pride of Jacob: "Surely I will never forget any of their deeds."

The word of the Lord. **Thanks be to God.**

Psalm 113

R. **Praise the Lord who lifts up the needy.**

or **Alleluia!**

Praise, O servants of the Lord;
praise the name of the Lord.
Blessed be the name of the Lord
from this time on and forevermore. R.

The Lord is high above all nations,
and his glory above the heavens.
Who is like the Lord our God, who is seated on high,
who looks far down on the heavens and the earth? R.

The Lord raises the poor from the dust,
and lifts the needy from the ash heap,
to make them sit with princes,
with the princes of his people. R.

A reading from the first Letter of Saint Paul to Timothy (2.1-7)

Beloved: I urge that supplications, prayers, intercessions, and thanksgivings be made for everyone, for kings and all who are in high positions, so that we may lead a quiet and peaceable life in all godliness and dignity. This is right and is acceptable in the sight of God our Saviour, who desires everyone to be saved and to come to the knowledge of the truth.

For there is one God; there is also one mediator between God and the human race, the man Christ Jesus, who gave himself a ransom for all; this was attested at the right time.

For this I was appointed a herald and an apostle, a teacher of the Gentiles in faith and truth. I am telling the truth, I am not lying.

The word of the Lord. **Thanks be to God.**

A reading from the holy Gospel according to Luke (16.1-13)

The shorter version begins at the asterisks.

Jesus said to the disciples, "There was a rich man who had a manager, and charges were brought to him that the manager was squandering his property. So the rich man summoned him and said to him, 'What is this that I hear about you? Give me an accounting of your management, because you cannot be my manager any longer.'

"Then the manager said to himself, 'What will I do, now that my master is taking the position away from me? I am not strong enough to dig, and I am ashamed to beg. I have decided what to do so that, when I am dismissed as manager, people may welcome me into their homes.'

"So, summoning his master's debtors one by one, he asked the first, 'How much do you owe my master?' He answered, 'A hundred jugs of olive oil.' He said to him, 'Take your bill, sit down quickly, and make it fifty.' Then he asked another, 'And how much do you owe?' He replied, 'A hundred containers of wheat.' He said to him, 'Take your bill and make it eighty.'

"And his master commended the dishonest manager because he had acted shrewdly; for the children of this age are more shrewd in dealing with their own generation than are the children of light.

"And I tell you, make friends for yourselves by means of dishonest wealth so that when it is gone, they may welcome you into the eternal homes.

* * *

"Whoever is faithful in a very little is faithful also in much; and whoever is dishonest in a very little is dishonest also in much. If then you have not been faithful with the dishonest wealth, who will entrust to you the true riches? And if you have not been faithful with what belongs to another, who will give you what is your own?

"No slave can serve two masters; for a slave will either hate the one and love the other, or be devoted to the one and despise the other. You cannot serve God and wealth."

The Gospel of the Lord.
Praise to you, Lord Jesus Christ.

Amos was a prophet and a friend of God. He lived 800 years before Jesus, at a time when rich people were very prosperous because they took advantage of the poor. The wealthy even bribed the judges. Amos spoke boldly to the rich and powerful, telling them this went against what God wanted.

Buying the poor, by making them work for wages so low that they cannot meet their basic needs, is taking advantage of them. God will not forget if his children are treated unjustly, for the Lord is as God of justice.

A mediator is someone who helps two people communicate in order to solve a dispute. Jesus, the Word of God, is our mediator so that humanity can encounter the true God without our human frailties getting in the way.

Apostle is a Greek word for "a person who is sent." The apostles were the twelve followers chosen by Jesus. Saint Paul also considered himself to be an apostle, even though he did not meet Jesus while Jesus was alive. Rather, Saint Paul encountered the risen Jesus on the road to Damascus.

To be faithful is to be honest and trustworthy, diligently carrying out whatever task we have been given.

September 29

26th Sunday in Ordinary Time

A reading from the book of the Prophet Amos (6.1, 4-7)

Thus says the Lord, the God of hosts: "Alas for those who are at ease in Zion, and for those who feel secure on Mount Samaria!

"Alas for those who lie on beds of ivory, and lounge on their couches, and eat lambs from the flock, and calves from the stall; who sing idle songs to the sound of the harp, and like David improvise on instruments of music; who drink wine from bowls, and anoint themselves with the finest oils, but are not grieved over the ruin of Joseph!

"Therefore they shall now be the first to go into exile, and the revelry of those who lie in ease shall pass away."

The word of the Lord. **Thanks be to God.**

Psalm 146

R. **Praise the Lord, O my soul!**

or **Alleluia!**

It is the Lord who keeps faith forever,
who executes justice for the oppressed;
who gives food to the hungry.
The Lord sets the prisoners free. R.

The Lord opens the eyes of the blind
and lifts up those who are bowed down;
the Lord loves the righteous
and watches over the strangers. R.

The Lord upholds the orphan and the widow,
but the way of the wicked he brings to ruin.
The Lord will reign forever,
your God, O Zion, for all generations. R.

A reading from the first Letter of Saint Paul to Timothy (6.11-16)

As for you, man of God; pursue righteousness, godliness, faith, love, endurance, gentleness. Fight the good fight of the faith; take hold of the eternal life, to which you were called and for which you made the good confession in the presence of many witnesses.

In the presence of God, who gives life to all things, and of Christ Jesus, who in his testimony before Pontius Pilate made the good confession, I charge you to keep the commandment without spot or blame until the manifestation of our Lord Jesus Christ, which he will bring about at the right time. He is the blessed and only Sovereign, the King of kings and Lord of lords.

It is he alone who has immortality and dwells in unapproachable light, whom no human being has ever seen or can see; to him be honour and eternal dominion. Amen.

The word of the Lord. **Thanks be to God.**

A reading from the holy Gospel according to Luke
(16.19-31)

Jesus told this parable to those among the Pharisees who loved money: "There was a rich man who was dressed in purple and fine linen and who feasted sumptuously every day. And at his gate lay a poor man named Lazarus, covered with sores, who longed to satisfy his hunger with what fell from the rich man's table; even the dogs would come and lick his sores.

"The poor man died and was carried away by the Angels to be with Abraham. The rich man also died and was buried. In Hades, where he was being tormented, he looked up and saw Abraham far away with Lazarus by his side. He called out, 'Father Abraham, have mercy on me, and send Lazarus to dip the tip of his finger in water and cool my tongue; for I am in agony in these flames.'

"But Abraham said, 'Child, remember that during your lifetime you received your good things, and Lazarus in like manner evil things; but now he is comforted here, and you are in agony. Besides all this, between you and us a great chasm has been fixed, so that those who might want to pass from here to you cannot do so, and no one can cross from there to us.'

"The man who had been rich said, 'Then, father, I beg you to send Lazarus to my father's house — for I have five brothers — that he may warn them, so that they will not also come into this place of torment.'

"Abraham replied, 'They have Moses and the Prophets; they should listen to them.' He said, 'No, father Abraham; but if someone goes to them from the dead, they will repent.' Abraham said to him, 'If they do not listen to Moses and the Prophets, neither will they be convinced even if someone rises from the dead.'"

The Gospel of the Lord. **Praise to you, Lord Jesus Christ.**

Alas is a word that means "too bad" or "shame." It is a way of saying things are not going to turn out well.

When someone is grieved they are brought to great sadness and thus moved to change their behaviour. The Prophet Amos warns the rich that they have hardened their hearts: they do not see the suffering and decay around them; they do not feel anything.

Revelry means celebrating and having a good time. Amos warns the rich that their days of thinking only of themselves are over; their wealth will not protect them from the anger of the Lord.

The call to gentleness is a call to respond without aggression when we are offended and humiliated. We must not act hastily, but with thought and care.

Saint Paul compares the mystery of God to a light so powerful and bright that we cannot stare at it or go near it — it is an unapproachable light. Even if we spend all our lives studying, we can never fully learn all there is to know about God.

For the Jews, people who lived good lives joined Abraham in heaven after they died. Abraham is the father of the Jewish faith.

Moses was the guide of the people when God liberated them from slavery in Egypt. When he ascended Mount Sinai, Moses received the task to transmit the law of God — the Ten Commandments — to everyone. To say "they have Moses" means that the people should pay attention to the Ten Commandments and the other things God told Moses.

October 6

27th Sunday in Ordinary Time

"O Lord, how long shall I cry for help,
and you will not listen?
Or cry to you 'Violence!'
and you will not save?
Why do you make me see wrongdoing
and look at trouble?
Destruction and violence are before me;
strife and contention arise."

Then the Lord answered me and said:
"Write the vision;
make it plain on tablets,
so that a runner may read it.
For there is still a vision for the appointed time;
it speaks of the end, and does not lie.
If it seems to tarry, wait for it;
it will surely come, it will not delay.
Look at the proud person!
Their spirit is not right in them,
but the righteous person lives by their faith."

The word of the Lord. **Thanks be to God.**

Psalm 95

R̶. **O that today you would listen to the voice of the Lord.
Do not harden your hearts!**

O come, let us sing to the Lord;
let us make a joyful noise to the rock of our salvation!
Let us come into his presence with thanksgiving;
let us make a joyful noise to him with songs of praise! R̶.

O come, let us worship and bow down,
let us kneel before the Lord, our Maker!
For he is our God, and we are the people of his pasture,
and the sheep of his hand. R̶.

O that today you would listen to his voice!
Do not harden your hearts, as at Meribah,
as on the day at Massah in the wilderness,
when your ancestors tested me,
and put me to the proof,
though they had seen my work. R̶.

A reading from the second Letter of Saint Paul to Timothy (1.6-8, 13-14)

Beloved: I remind you to rekindle the gift of God that is within you through the laying on of my hands; for God did not give us a spirit of cowardice, but rather a spirit of power and of love and of self-discipline. Do not be ashamed, then, of the testimony about our Lord or of me his prisoner, but join with me in suffering for the Gospel, relying on the power of God.

Hold to the standard of sound teaching that you have heard from me, in the faith and love that are in Christ Jesus. Guard the good treasure entrusted to you, with the help of the Holy Spirit living in us.

The word of the Lord. **Thanks be to God.**

A reading from the holy Gospel according to Luke (17.5-10)

The Apostles said to the Lord, "Increase our faith!" The Lord replied, "If you had faith the size of a mustard seed, you could say to this mulberry tree, 'Be uprooted and planted in the sea,' and it would obey you.

"Who among you would say to your slave who has just come in from ploughing or tending sheep in the field, 'Come here at once and take your place at the table'? Would you not rather say to him, 'Prepare supper for me, put on your apron and serve me while I eat and drink; later you may eat and drink'? Do you thank the slave for doing what was commanded? So you also, when you have done all that you were ordered to do, say, 'We are worthless slaves; we have done only what we ought to have done!'"

The Gospel of the Lord.
Praise to you, Lord Jesus Christ.

Habakkuk was a prophet who lived at the end of the seventh century before Christ. He was an unusual prophet, because he openly questioned the wisdom of God when he saw all the suffering endured by God's people. Habakkuk, nevertheless, taught the people to hope in God and to believe in God's promises.

Habakkuk felt that God was not listening to his prayer. Nevertheless, he believed God was there and he continued to cry out, "Will you not listen?" until God responded with a message of hope.

When we bow down we adopt a posture that shows reverence towards God. It is a way for us to acknowledge that we are before our Creator and Lord.

The laying on of hands was a gesture used by Saint Paul and other apostles in order to pass on the Holy Spirit to new Christians. This gesture is still used when priests are ordained, in the sacrament of Confirmation, when we pray over the sick, and when we give a blessing.

A person exercises self-discipline when they learn to use all things without excess. We can, for example, eat, have fun, relax — but in moderation. This way, we honour God's gifts without bringing harm to ourselves or others.

A testimony is a word or example given so that others may be convinced of something. For example, the martyrs were Christians who offered their lives in testimony or witness so that others would believe in Jesus.

The apostles asked Jesus to "increase our faith." Our faith is a gift from God that will increase through prayer, study, the sacraments, and love of our neighbour.

October 13

28th Sunday in Ordinary Time

A reading from the second book of Kings (5.14-17)

Naaman the Syrian went down and immersed himself seven times in the Jordan, according to the word of the man of God; his flesh was restored like the flesh of a young boy, and he was clean.

Then he returned to the man of God, he and all his company; Naaman came and stood before Elisha and said, "Now I know that there is no God in all the earth except in Israel; please accept a present from your servant."

But Elisha said, "As the Lord lives, whom I serve, I will accept nothing!" Naaman urged Elisha to accept, but he refused.

Then Naaman said, "If not, please let two mule-loads of earth be given to your servant; for your servant will no longer offer burnt offering or sacrifice to any god except the Lord."

The word of the Lord. **Thanks be to God.**

Psalm 98

R. **The Lord has revealed his victory**
in the sight of the nations.

O sing to the Lord a new song,
for he has done marvellous things.
His right hand and his holy arm
have brought him victory. R.

The Lord has made known his victory;
he has revealed his vindication in the sight of the nations.
He has remembered his steadfast love
and faithfulness to the house of Israel. R.

All the ends of the earth have seen
the victory of our God.
Make a joyful noise to the Lord, all the earth;
break forth into joyous song and sing praises. R.

A reading from the second Letter of Saint Paul to Timothy (2.8-13)

Beloved: Remember Jesus Christ, raised from the dead, a descendant of David — that is my Gospel, for which I suffer hardship, even to the point of being chained like a criminal. But the word of God is not chained.

Therefore I endure everything for the sake of the elect, so that they may also obtain the salvation that is in Christ Jesus, with eternal glory.

The saying is sure: If we have died with him, we will also live with him; if we endure, we will also reign with him; if we deny him, he will also deny us; if we are faithless, he remains faithful — for he cannot deny himself.

The word of the Lord. **Thanks be to God.**

A reading from the holy Gospel according to Luke (17.11-19)

On the way to Jerusalem Jesus was going through the region between Samaria and Galilee.

As he entered a village, ten lepers approached him. Keeping their distance, they called out, saying, "Jesus, Master, have mercy on us!"

When Jesus saw them, he said to them, "Go and show yourselves to the priests." And as they went, they were made clean. Then one of them, when he saw that he was healed, turned back, praising God with a loud voice. He prostrated himself at Jesus' feet and thanked him. And he was a Samaritan.

Then Jesus asked, "Were not ten made clean? But the other nine, where are they? Was none of them found to return and give praise to God except this foreigner?"

Then Jesus said to the Samaritan, "Get up and go on your way; your faith has made you well."

The Gospel of the Lord.
**Praise to you,
Lord Jesus Christ.**

In the Bible the two books of Kings tell the story of a time when Israel was ruled by kings. The books begin with the death of King David, nearly 1,000 years before Jesus was born, and end when the Babylonians capture Jerusalem, nearly 600 years before Jesus. The writer wants us to see how God helped his people throughout history.

God told Elijah to anoint Elisha to be prophet after him, in order to guide the people so they would not stray from God. Elisha lived about 850 years before Jesus.

David was the second king of Israel, from the year 1010 to 970 before Christ. David was said to have musical talent, and was the hero who killed the giant Goliath. Although he committed serious errors during his reign, God forgave him. In all, he was a good king, well-loved by the people.

The word Gospel means a message that communicates good news. There are four Gospels in the Bible, written by Saints Matthew, Mark, Luke and John. The word "Gospel" also means the good news that Jesus rose from the dead.

People who suffered from Hansen's disease or leprosy always were keeping their distance from healthy people because they believed they would infect them if they came too near. This meant that lepers had to live far outside the village limits.

Lepers who believed they were cured had to show themselves to the priests so that they could be assured they were healthy again. The priests would decide whether or not they could return to live among the people.

Samaritans were people who came from Samaria, a region of Israel to the south of Galilee and to the north of Judea. See map on page 328. Jews and Samaritans did not talk to each other because of historical differences. It is astonishing that the only leper to say thankyou to Jesus was a Samaritan.

29th Sunday In Ordinary Time

A reading from the book of Exodus (17.8-13)

Amalek came and fought with Israel at Rephidim. Moses said to Joshua, "Choose some men for us and go out, fight with Amalek. Tomorrow I will stand on the top of the hill with the staff of God in my hand."

So Joshua did as Moses told him, and fought with Amalek, while Moses, Aaron, and Hur went up to the top of the hill.

Whenever Moses held up his hands, Israel prevailed; and whenever he lowered his hands, Amalek prevailed. But Moses' hands grew weary; so they took a stone and put it under him, and he sat on it. Aaron and Hur held up his hands, one on one side, and the other on the other side; so his hands were steady until the sun set.

And Joshua defeated Amalek and his people with the sword.

The word of the Lord. **Thanks be to God.**

Psalm 121

R. **Our help is from the Lord, who made heaven and earth.**

I lift up my eyes to the hills —
from where will my help come?
My help comes from the Lord,
who made heaven and earth. R.

The Lord will not let your foot be moved;
he who keeps you will not slumber.
He who keeps Israel
will neither slumber nor sleep. R.

The Lord is your keeper;
the Lord is your shade at your right hand.
The sun shall not strike you by day,
nor the moon by night. R.

The Lord will keep you from all evil;
he will keep your life.
The Lord will keep your going out and your coming in
from this time on and forevermore. R.

A reading from the second Letter of Saint Paul to Timothy (3.14 – 4.2)

Beloved: Continue in what you have learned and firmly believed, knowing from whom you learned it, and how from childhood you have known the sacred writings that are able to instruct you for salvation through faith in Christ Jesus.

All Scripture is inspired by God and is useful for teaching, for reproof, for correction, and for training in righteousness, so that the one who belongs to God may be proficient, equipped for every good work.

In the presence of God and of Christ Jesus, who is to judge the living and the dead, and in view of his appearing and his kingdom, I solemnly urge you: proclaim the message; be persistent whether the time is favourable or unfavourable; convince, rebuke, and encourage, with the utmost patience in teaching.

The word of the Lord. **Thanks be to God.**

A reading from the holy Gospel according to Luke (18.1-8)

Jesus told the disciples a parable about their need to pray always and not to lose heart.

He said, "In a certain city there was a judge who neither feared God nor had respect for any human being. In that city there was a widow who kept coming to him and saying, 'Grant me justice against my opponent.'

"For a while the judge refused; but later he said to himself, 'Though I have no fear of God and no respect for any human being, yet because this widow keeps bothering me, I will grant her justice, so that she may not wear me out by continually coming.'"

And the Lord said, "Listen to what the unjust judge says. Will not God grant justice to his chosen ones who cry to him day and night? Will he delay long in helping them? I tell you, God will quickly grant justice to them. And yet, when the Son of Man comes, will he find faith on earth?"

The Gospel of the Lord.
Praise to you, Lord Jesus Christ.

KEY WORDS

The Amalekites were a tribe led by Amalek that lived to the south of Palestine. Although they were descended from Abraham, they were long-time enemies of Israel. The Israelites had to conquer them in order to reach the Promised Land.

The staff of God was a sign of authority that Moses had over the people of Israel. In our times we still use similar symbols to show that God has given a person the authority to help others. The pope and bishops, for example, in some ceremonies, use the crozier (a tall staff) as a sign that they are shepherds who guide us Christians.

A man named Hosea was chosen by Moses to help him lead the people of Israel to the Promised Land. Moses then changed his name to Joshua. Moses died before they arrived, so it was Joshua who led the Israelites in their struggle to enter the Promised Land.

Timothy was a companion of Saint Paul. He helped Paul to spread the Gospel and at one time was thrown into jail with his master. In the New Testament there are two letters to Timothy, where Saint Paul gives him advice as the person responsible (bishop) for the Church in Ephesus.

Jesus is always with us when we gather in community, when we read the word of God, when we celebrate the Eucharist, and when we help someone who is in need. Nevertheless, Saint Paul and the early Christians yearned for the appearing of Christ among them. Jesus promised that he would come back to us at the end of time when history reaches its fullness.

A widow is a woman whose husband has died. At the time of Jesus, when a woman married her husband, she left her own family and became part of her husband's family. When he died, she was left without anyone to care for her or protect her, leaving her among the poor and powerless of the community.

October 27

30th Sunday in Ordinary Time

The Lord is the judge, and with him there is no partiality. He will not show partiality to the poor but he will listen to the prayer of one who is wronged. The Lord will not ignore the supplication of the orphan, or the widow when she pours out her complaint.

The person whose service is pleasing to the Lord will be accepted, and their prayer will reach to the clouds.

The prayer of the humble pierces the clouds, and it will not rest until it reaches its goal; it will not desist until the Most High responds and does justice for the righteous, and executes judgment. Indeed, the Lord will not delay.

The word of the Lord. **Thanks be to God.**

Psalm 34

R. **The poor one called and the Lord heard.**

I will bless the Lord at all times;
his praise shall continually be in my mouth.
My soul makes its boast in the Lord;
let the humble hear and be glad. R.

The face of the Lord is against evildoers,
to cut off the remembrance of them from the earth.
When the righteous cry for help, the Lord hears,
and rescues them from all their troubles. R.

The Lord is near to the broken-hearted,
and saves the crushed in spirit.
The Lord redeems the life of his servants;
none of those who take refuge in him will be condemned. R.

A reading from the second Letter of Saint Paul to Timothy (4.6-8, 16-18)

Beloved: I am already being poured out as a libation, and the time of my departure has come. I have fought the good fight, I have finished the race, I have kept the faith.

From now on there is reserved for me the crown of righteousness, which the Lord, the righteous judge, will give me on that day, and not only to me but also to all who have longed for his appearing.

At my first defence no one came to my support, but all deserted me. May it not be counted against them!

But the Lord stood by me and gave me strength, so that through me the message might be fully proclaimed and all the Gentiles might hear it. So I was rescued from the lion's mouth.

The Lord will rescue me from every evil attack and save me for his heavenly kingdom. To him be the glory forever and ever. Amen.

The word of the Lord. **Thanks be to God.**

A reading from the holy Gospel according to Luke (18.9-14)

Jesus told this parable to some who trusted in themselves that they were righteous, and regarded others with contempt:

"Two men went up to the temple to pray, one a Pharisee and the other a tax collector. The Pharisee, standing by himself, was praying thus, 'God, I thank you that I am not like other people: thieves, rogues, adulterers, or even like this tax collector. I fast twice a week; I give a tenth of all my income.'

"But the tax collector, standing far off, would not even look up to heaven, but was beating his breast and saying, 'God, be merciful to me, a sinner!'

"I tell you, this man went down to his home justified rather than the other; for whoever exalts himself will be humbled, but whoever humbles himself will be exalted."

The Gospel of the Lord. **Praise to you, Lord Jesus Christ.**

A judge is someone who is called to make decisions without partiality, that is, without showing special favours but treating everyone equally and with fairness. Sirach believes God to be a just and fair judge.

A supplication is a cry or plea for something we need. When we pray, our prayer can be a supplication if we have something special to ask of God.

To desist from something is to stop or hold back from doing something. We are reminded to be persistent in our prayer and not to desist in bringing to God our needs and cares.

A libation is a special drink that is poured out as an offering. Saint Paul uses this wonderful image to describe his life in service of the Gospel — he is pouring his life out as an offering to God.

A parable is a story that carries a deeper meaning beyond the obvious. Jesus used many parables in his teaching, because the people found the stories interesting and could more easily learn from them.

Rogues are rough men who are trouble-makers. The Pharisee would not be happy to see rogues in the temple. Through this parable Jesus shows us that God looks into our hearts and does not judge us solely on our outward actions.

To exalt someone is to praise or elevate them to a higher level. In today's parable, Jesus cautions against exalting ourselves or being overly proud of ourselves. A true humility is our proper stance before God.

November 3

31st Sunday in Ordinary Time

The whole world before you, O Lord,
is like a speck that tips the scales,
and like a drop of morning dew that falls on the ground.
But you are merciful to all,
for you can do all things,
and you overlook people's sins,
so that they may repent.

Lord, you love all things that exist,
and detest none of the things that you have made,
for you would not have made anything if you had hated it.
How would anything have endured
if you had not willed it?
Or how would anything not called forth by you
have been preserved?
You spare all things, for they are yours, O Lord,
you who love the living.

For your immortal spirit is in all things.
Therefore you correct little by little those who trespass,
and you remind and warn them of the things
    through which they sin,
so that they may be freed from wickedness
and put their trust in you, O Lord.

The word of the Lord. **Thanks be to God.**

R̶. **I will bless your name for ever, my King and my God.**

I will extol you, my God and King,
and bless your name forever and ever.
Every day I will bless you,
and praise your name forever and ever. R̶.

The Lord is gracious and merciful,
slow to anger and abounding in steadfast love.
The Lord is good to all,
and his compassion is over all that he has made. R̶.

All your works shall give thanks to you, O Lord,
and all your faithful shall bless you.
They shall speak of the glory of your kingdom,
and tell of your power. R̶.

The Lord is faithful in all his words,
and gracious in all his deeds.
The Lord upholds all who are falling,
and raises up all who are bowed down. R̶.

A reading from the second Letter of Saint Paul to the Thessalonians (1.11 – 2.2)

Brothers and sisters: We always pray for you, asking that our God will make you worthy of his call and will fulfill by his power every good resolve and work of faith, so that the name of our Lord Jesus may be glorified in you, and you in him, according to the grace of our God and the Lord Jesus Christ.

As to the coming of our Lord Jesus Christ and our being gathered together to him, we beg you, brothers and sisters, not to be quickly shaken in mind or alarmed, either by spirit or by word or by letter, as though from us, to the effect that the day of the Lord is already here.

The word of the Lord. **Thanks be to God.**

Jesus entered Jericho and was passing through it. A man was there named Zacchaeus; he was a chief tax collector and was rich. He was trying to see who Jesus was, but on account of the crowd he could not, because he was short in stature.

So he ran ahead and climbed a sycamore tree to see Jesus, because he was going to pass that way. When Jesus came to the place, he looked up and said to him, "Zacchaeus, hurry and come down; for I must stay at your house today."

So Zacchaeus hurried down and was happy to welcome Jesus. All who saw it began to grumble and said, "He has gone to be the guest of one who is a sinner."

Zacchaeus stood there and said to the Lord, "Look, half of my possessions, Lord, I will give to the poor; and if I have defrauded anyone of anything, I will pay back four times as much."

Then Jesus said of him, "Today salvation has come to this house, because Zacchaeus too is a son of Abraham. For the Son of Man came to seek out and to save the lost."

The Gospel of the Lord.
Praise to you,
Lord Jesus Christ.

When we make mistakes and do things that distance us from friendship with God, God always gives us a chance to repent or say we are sorry. God loves us and forgives us when we know we have done wrong.

To extol the qualities of someone is to recognize and praise their virtues. When we pray to God, the first thing we should do is praise or extol God for his goodness and love, before we ask God for something special.

When we live the life Jesus has planned for us, we are responding to his call. God makes us aware in our hearts of his invitation to follow him in service of others.

Saint Paul tells the Thessalonians not to pay attention to people who were trying to scare them with thoughts that the world was about to end. The day of the Lord, or the end of time, is when Jesus will come again, and it is not a day to be feared but to be welcomed.

Jericho was an important city near Jerusalem in what is now called the West Bank. In the book of Exodus, Joshua won a great victory at Jericho after the parting of the Red Sea. It was near Jericho that Jesus cured the blind man Bartimaeus, who had cried out, "Son of David, have mercy on me!" As well, the Good Samaritan was travelling on the road from Jerusalem to Jericho when he found the man who had been attacked by robbers.

November 10

32nd Sunday in Ordinary Time

It happened that seven brothers and their mother were arrested and were being compelled by King Antiochus, under torture with whips and thongs, to partake of unlawful swine's flesh. One of the brothers, speaking for all, said, "What do you intend to ask and learn from us? For we are ready to die rather than transgress the laws of our ancestors."

After the first brother had died, they brought forward the second for their sport. And when he was at his last breath, he said to King, "You accursed wretch, you dismiss us from this present life, but the King of the universe will raise us up to an everlasting renewal of life, because we have died for his laws."

After him, the third was the victim of their sport. When it was demanded, he quickly put out his tongue and courageously stretched forth his hands, and said nobly, "I got these from Heaven, and because of God's laws I disdain them, and from God I hope to get them back again."

As a result the king himself and those with him were astonished at the young man's spirit, for he regarded his sufferings as nothing.

After the third brother too had died, they maltreated and tortured the fourth in the same way. When he was near death, he said to his torturers, "One cannot but choose to die at the hands of humans and to cherish the hope God gives of being raised by him. But for you, there will be no resurrection to life!"

The word of the Lord. **Thanks be to God.**

R. **I shall be satisfied, Lord,**
when I awake and behold your likeness.

Hear a just cause, O Lord;
attend to my cry;
give ear to my prayer
from lips free of deceit. R.

My steps have held fast to your paths;
my feet have not slipped.
I call upon you, for you will answer me, O God;
incline your ear to me, hear my words. R.

Guard me as the apple of the eye;
hide me in the shadow of your wings,
As for me, I shall behold your face in righteousness;
when I awake I shall be satisfied,
beholding your likeness. R.

A reading from the second Letter of Saint Paul to the Thessalonians (2.16 – 3.5)

Brothers and sisters: May our Lord Jesus Christ himself and God our Father, who loved us and through grace gave us eternal comfort and good hope, comfort your hearts and strengthen them in every good work and word.

Brothers and sisters, pray for us, so that the word of the Lord may spread rapidly and be glorified everywhere, just as it is among you, and that we may be rescued from wicked and evil people; for not all have faith.

But the Lord is faithful; he will strengthen you and guard you from the evil one. And we have confidence in the Lord concerning you, that you are doing and will go on doing the things that we command. May the Lord direct your hearts to the love of God and to the steadfastness of Christ.

The word of the Lord. **Thanks be to God.**

For the shorter version, omit the indented part.

Some Sadducees, those who say there is no resurrection, came to Jesus.

> and asked him a question, "Teacher, Moses wrote for us that if a man's brother dies, leaving a wife but no children, the man shall marry the widow and raise up children for his brother. Now there were seven brothers; the first married, and died childless; then the second and the third married her, and so in the same way all seven died childless.
>
> Finally the woman also died. In the resurrection, therefore, whose wife will the woman be? — for the seven had married her."

Jesus said to them, "The children of this age marry and are given in marriage; but those who are considered worthy of a place in that age and in the resurrection from the dead neither marry nor are given in marriage. Indeed they cannot die any more, because they are like Angels and are sons and daughters of God, being children of the resurrection.

"And the fact that the dead are raised Moses himself showed in the story about the bush, where he speaks of the Lord as the God of Abraham, the God of Isaac, and the God of Jacob. Now he is God not of the dead, but of the living; for to him all of them are alive."

The Gospel of the Lord.
Praise to you, Lord Jesus Christ.

The two books of the Bible called Maccabees tell the story of how Judas Maccabee ("the Hammer") and his brothers rose up against the king of Syria who was dominating the Hebrews. They were able to win back religious liberty for the Jews 160 years before Christ. The Jewish festival of Hanukkah commemorates this great event.

It is against the laws of Judaism to eat pork or swine's flesh. For the Maccabees, to be forced to eat pork was the worst kind of torture, for they would be disobeying God. The brothers were prepared to die rather than be unfaithful to God.

Saint Paul wrote two letters to the Thessalonians (people living in Thessalonika) — a community that Saint Paul himself had converted. In the first letter, Paul comforts them by saying that there is no need to be afraid for loved ones who have died, because the Lord will raise them. In the second letter Paul tells them that since the end of the world is not near, they should continuing working for the Lord.

At the time of Jesus, there were groups among the Jews such as the Pharisees and Sadducees. The Sadducees were very important, because they were responsible for the Temple — making sacrifices, performing priestly duties, and taking care of the building. They did not believe in a resurrection after death, which made them different from the Pharisees and the early Christians.

It is not easy to imagine what our life will be like after the resurrection from the dead, because it will be a totally different life. We know that it will not be the same as this world — we will live in great joy as children of God, reunited with all our loved ones.

November 17

33rd Sunday in Ordinary Time

A reading from the book of the Prophet Malachi (4.1-2)

"See, the day is coming, burning like an oven,
when all the arrogant and all evildoers will be stubble;
the day that comes shall burn them up," says the Lord of hosts,
"so that it will leave them neither root nor branch.

"But for you who revere my name
the sun of righteousness shall rise,
with healing in its wings."

The word of the Lord. **Thanks be to God.**

Psalm 98

R̗ **The Lord is coming to judge the peoples with equity.**

Sing praises to the Lord with the lyre,
with the lyre and the sound of melody.
With trumpets and the sound of the horn
make a joyful noise before the King, the Lord. R̗

Let the sea roar, and all that fills it;
the world and those who live in it.
Let the floods clap their hands;
let the hills sing together for joy
   at the presence of the Lord. R̗

For the Lord is coming,
coming to judge the earth.
He will judge the world with righteousness,
and the peoples with equity. R̗

A reading from the second Letter of Saint Paul to the Thessalonians (3.7-12)

Brothers and sisters, you yourselves know how you ought to imitate us; we were not idle when we were with you, and we did not eat anyone's bread without paying for it; but with toil and labour we worked night and day, so that we might not burden any of you.

This was not because we do not have that right, but in order to give you an example to imitate. For even when we were with you, we gave you this command: "Anyone unwilling to work should not eat."

For we hear that some of you are living in idleness, mere busybodies, not doing any work. Now such persons we command and exhort in the Lord Jesus Christ to do their work quietly and to earn their own living.

The word of the Lord. **Thanks be to God.**

A reading from the holy Gospel according to Luke
(21.5-19)

When some were speaking about the temple, how it was adorned with beautiful stones and gifts dedicated to God, Jesus said, "As for these things that you see, the days will come when not one stone will be left upon another; all will be thrown down."

They asked him, "Teacher, when will this be, and what will be the sign that this is about to take place?"

And Jesus said, "Beware that you are not led astray; for many will come in my name and say, 'I am he!' and, 'The time is near!' Do not go after them.

"When you hear of wars and insurrections, do not be terrified; for these things must take place first, but the end will not follow immediately."

Then Jesus said to them, "Nation will rise against nation, and kingdom against kingdom; there will be great earthquakes, and in various places famines and plagues; and there will be dreadful portents and great signs from heaven.

"But before all this occurs, they will arrest you and persecute you; they will hand you over to synagogues and prisons, and you will be brought before kings and governors because of my name.

"This will give you an opportunity to testify. So make up your minds not to prepare your defence in advance; for I will give you words and a wisdom that none of your opponents will be able to withstand or contradict.

"You will be betrayed even by parents, by brothers and sisters, and by relatives and friends; and they will put some of you to death. You will be hated by all because of my name. But not a hair of your head will perish. By your endurance you will gain your souls."

The Gospel of the Lord. **Praise to you, Lord Jesus Christ.**

The phrase "the day is coming" refers to the last day of history at the end of time when God will come to judge the living and the dead.

In the Bible, God is referred to as the Lord of hosts — a host being a large army or group. This title makes it clear that God is more powerful than all human power. He is master and lord of all.

The Gospel of Saint Luke was written for Christians who were not Jewish before becoming Christian. It is also known as the Gospel of mercy. The Acts of the Apostles was also written by Saint Luke.

We are warned not to believe those who say, "I am he!" or to be led astray by others who would have us believe that they can save us. There is only one Saviour and Lord Jesus Christ.

At the time Saint Luke wrote his Gospel, the early Christians were being persecuted or oppressed because of their faith in Jesus. Luke sought to give them hope at a difficult time.

Jesus made a promise to his followers that "not a hair of your head will perish." It means that although we may pass through difficult moments, and although many Christians have lost their lives for the cause of the faith (such as the martyrs), nothing can happen that will lessen the love God has for us.

November 24

Our Lord Jesus Christ, King of the Universe (Christ the King)

A reading from the second book of Samuel (5.1-3)

All the tribes of Israel came to David at Hebron, and said, "Look, we are your bone and flesh. For some time, while Saul was king over us, it was you who led out Israel and brought it in. The Lord said to you: 'It is you who shall be shepherd of my people Israel, you who shall be ruler over Israel.'"

So all the elders of Israel came to the king at Hebron; and King David made a covenant with them at Hebron before the Lord, and they anointed David king over Israel.

The word of the Lord. **Thanks be to God.**

Psalm 122

℟. **Let us go rejoicing to the house of the Lord.**

I was glad when they said to me,
"Let us go to the house of the Lord!"
Our feet are standing
within your gates, O Jerusalem. ℟.

Jerusalem — built as a city
that is bound firmly together.
To it the tribes go up,
the tribes of the Lord. ℟.

As was decreed for Israel,
to give thanks to the name of the Lord.
For there the thrones for judgment were set up,
the thrones of the house of David. ℟.

A reading from the Letter of Saint Paul to the Colossians (1.12-20)

Brothers and sisters: Give thanks to the Father, who has enabled you to share in the inheritance of the saints in the light. The Father has rescued us from the power of darkness and transferred us into the kingdom of his beloved Son, in whom we have redemption, the forgiveness of sins.

Christ is the image of the invisible God, the firstborn of all creation; for in him all things in heaven and on earth were created, things visible and invisible, whether thrones or dominions or rulers or powers — all things have been created through him and for him. Christ is before all things, and in him all things hold together.

He is the head of the body, the Church; he is the beginning, the firstborn from the dead, so that he might come to have first place in everything. For in Christ all the fullness of God was pleased to dwell, and through him God was pleased to reconcile to himself all things, whether on earth or in heaven, by making peace through the blood of his Cross.

The word of the Lord. **Thanks be to God.**

A reading from the holy Gospel according to Luke (23.35-43)

The leaders scoffed at Jesus saying, "He saved others; let him save himself if he is the Christ of God, his chosen one!" The soldiers also mocked Jesus, coming up and offering him sour wine, and saying, "If you are the King of the Jews, save yourself!" There was also an inscription over him, "This is the King of the Jews."

One of the criminals who were hanged there kept deriding him and saying, "Are you not the Christ? Save yourself and us!"

But the other rebuked him, saying, "Do you not fear God, since you are under the same sentence of condemnation? And we indeed have been condemned justly, for we are getting what we deserve for our deeds, but this man has done nothing wrong." Then he said, "Jesus, remember me when you come into your kingdom." Jesus replied, "Truly I tell you, today you will be with me in Paradise."

The Gospel of the Lord. **Praise to you, Lord Jesus Christ.**

The Solemnity of Christ the King brings the liturgical year to a close. It is like New Year's Eve, with a new liturgical year beginning next Sunday, the First Sunday of Advent.

The tribes of Israel were groups of families or clans descended from Jacob. Israel was formed by the union of 12 tribes each known by the name of their founder: all sons of Jacob.

The elders anointed David king by pouring oil over his head in a ceremony in front of all the people. The new king, Jesus, is named "the anointed one" (the Christ) because after he rose from the dead his disciples realized that he was the true king.

Saint Paul wrote a letter to the Colossians, members of a Christian community in the town of Colossae (in modern-day Turkey). They were doubting their faith, but Paul's letter encouraged them to be strong and reminded them that Jesus comes before everything else.

By sin, humanity lost friendship with God, but because the Son of God died for our sins, God reconciled us to himself. We regained God's friendship.

On many crucifixes there is a small sign above Jesus with the letters, INRI. These letters stand for Iesus Nazarenus Rex Iudaeorum which is Latin for "Jesus of Nazareth, King of the Jews."

1st Sunday of Advent

A reading from the book of the Prophet Isaiah (2.1-5)

The word that Isaiah son of Amoz saw concerning Judah and Jerusalem. In days to come the mountain of the Lord's house shall be established as the highest of the mountains, and shall be raised above the hills; all the nations shall stream to it.

Many peoples shall come and say, "Come, let us go up to the mountain of the Lord, to the house of the God of Jacob; that he may teach us his ways and that we may walk in his paths."

For out of Zion shall go forth instruction, and the word of the Lord from Jerusalem. He shall judge between the nations, and shall arbitrate for many peoples; they shall beat their swords into ploughshares, and their spears into pruning hooks; nation shall not lift up sword against nation, neither shall they learn war any more.

O house of Jacob, come, let us walk in the light of the Lord!

The word of the Lord. **Thanks be to God.**

Psalm 122

R. **Let us go rejoicing to the house of the Lord.**

I was glad when they said to me,
"Let us go to the house of the Lord!"
Our feet are standing
within your gates, O Jerusalem. R.

To it the tribes go up, the tribes of the Lord,
as was decreed for Israel, to give thanks
    to the name of the Lord.
For there the thrones for judgment were set up,
the thrones of the house of David. R.

Pray for the peace of Jerusalem:
"May they prosper who love you.
Peace be within your walls,
and security within your towers." R.

For the sake of my relatives and friends
I will say, "Peace be within you."
For the sake of the house of the Lord our God,
I will seek your good. R.

Brothers and sisters, you know what time it is, how it is now the moment for you to wake from sleep. For salvation is nearer to us now than when we became believers; the night is far gone, the day is near. Let us then lay aside the works of darkness and put on the armour of light; let us live honourably as in the day, not in revelling and drunkenness, not in debauchery and licentiousness, not in quarrelling and jealousy.

Instead, put on the Lord Jesus Christ, and make no provision for the flesh, to gratify its desires.

The word of the Lord. **Thanks be to God.**

A reading from the holy Gospel according to Matthew
(24.37-44)

Jesus spoke to his disciples: "As the days of Noah were, so will be the coming of the Son of Man. For as in those days before the flood they were eating and drinking, marrying and giving in marriage, until the day Noah entered the ark, and they knew nothing until the flood came and swept them all away, so too will be the coming of the Son of Man. Then two will be in the field; one will be taken and one will be left. Two women will be grinding meal together; one will be taken and one will be left.

"Keep awake, therefore, for you do not know on what day your Lord is coming. But understand this: if the owner of the house had known in what part of the night the thief was coming, he would have stayed awake and would not have let his house be broken into. Therefore you also must be ready, for the Son of Man is coming at an unexpected hour."

The Gospel of the Lord.
Praise to you, Lord Jesus Christ.

295

When the prophet Isaiah spoke of the mountain of the Lord's house, he was referring to the temple of Jerusalem. With this phrase he wanted to teach that there will come a time when the God of Israel will be known and reverenced by all the people of the world.

Jacob was a grandson of Abraham and the father of twelve sons, after whom the twelve tribes of Israel were named. So, the house of Jacob was a way to refer to all the people of Israel. Jacob died in Egypt, where his son Joseph grew to be a close friend and very important advisor to Pharaoh.

The works of darkness are bad actions that break our friendship with God and other people.

The armour of light is the willingness and desire to follow the teachings of Jesus. To be friends of Jesus we must be ready to struggle against all that might distance us from God.

Noah was the just man chosen by God to be saved from the flood, along with his family and two of every animal. God asked Noah to build a huge boat, called an ark, in which he, his family and the animals would live during the flood.

To keep awake is to avoid sleep throughout the night. But it also means being attentive so that nothing can surprise us. Christians must live in such a way that we're ready at any moment to meet our Lord.

December 8

2nd Sunday of Advent

On that day:
A shoot shall come out from the stump of Jesse,
and a branch shall grow out of his roots.
The spirit of the Lord shall rest on him,
the spirit of wisdom and understanding,
the spirit of counsel and might,
the spirit of knowledge and the fear of the Lord.
His delight shall be in the fear of the Lord.

He shall not judge by what his eyes see,
or decide by what his ears hear;
but with righteousness he shall judge the poor,
and decide with equity for the meek of the earth;
he shall strike the earth with the rod of his mouth,
and with the breath of his lips he shall kill the wicked.
Righteousness shall be the belt around his waist,
and faithfulness the belt around his loins.

The wolf shall live with the lamb,
the leopard shall lie down with the kid,
the calf and the lion and the fatling together,
and a little child shall lead them.
The cow and the bear shall graze,
their young shall lie down together;
and the lion shall eat straw like the ox.
The nursing child shall play over the hole of the asp,
and the weaned child shall put its hand on the adder's den.
They will not hurt or destroy
on all my holy mountain;
for the earth will be full of the knowledge of the Lord
as the waters cover the sea.

On that day the root of Jesse shall stand
as a signal to the peoples;
the nations shall inquire of him,
and his dwelling shall be glorious.

The word of the Lord. **Thanks be to God.**

R. **In his days may righteousness flourish,
and peace abound forever.**

Give the king your justice, O God,
and your righteousness to a king's son.
May he judge your people with righteousness,
and your poor with justice. R.

In his days may righteousness flourish
and peace abound, until the moon is no more.
May he have dominion from sea to sea,
and from the River to the ends of the earth. R.

For he delivers the needy one who calls,
the poor and the one who has no helper.
He has pity on the weak and the needy,
and saves the lives of the needy. R.

May his name endure forever,
his fame continue as long as the sun.
May all nations be blessed in him;
may they pronounce him happy. R.

A reading from the Letter of Saint Paul to the Romans (15.4-9)

Brothers and sisters: Whatever was written in former days was written for our instruction, so that by steadfastness and by the encouragement of the Scriptures we might have hope.

May the God of steadfastness and encouragement grant you to live in harmony with one another, in accordance with Christ Jesus, so that together you may with one voice glorify the God and Father of our Lord Jesus Christ.

Welcome one another, therefore, just as Christ has welcomed you, for the glory of God. For I tell you that Christ has become a servant of the circumcised on behalf of the truth of God in order that he might confirm the promises given to the patriarchs, and in order that the Gentiles might glorify God for his mercy. As it is written, "Therefore I will confess you among the Gentiles, and sing praises to your name."

The word of the Lord. **Thanks be to God.**

In those days John the Baptist appeared in the wilderness of Judea, proclaiming, "Repent, for the kingdom of heaven has come near." This is the one of whom the Prophet Isaiah spoke when he said, "The voice of one crying out in the wilderness: 'Prepare the way of the Lord, make his paths straight.'"

Now John wore clothing of camel's hair with a leather belt around his waist, and his food was locusts and wild honey. Then the people of Jerusalem and all Judea were going out to him, and all the region along the Jordan, and they were baptized by him in the river Jordan, confessing their sins.

But when he saw many Pharisees and Sadducees coming for baptism, John said to them, "You brood of vipers! Who warned you to flee from the wrath to come? Bear fruit worthy of repentance. Do not presume to say to yourselves, 'We have Abraham as our father'; for I tell you, God is able from these stones to raise up children to Abraham. Even now the axe is lying at the root of the trees; every tree therefore that does not bear good fruit is cut down and thrown into the fire.

"I baptize you with water for repentance, but one who is more powerful than I is coming after me; I am not worthy to carry his sandals. He will baptize you with the Holy Spirit and fire. His winnowing fork is in his hand, and he will clear his threshing floor and will gather his wheat into the granary; but the chaff he will burn with unquenchable fire."

The Gospel of the Lord.
Praise to you, Lord Jesus Christ.

The prophet Isaiah was making a comparison between a branch that seemed withered and dead, and the hope of the people. When he referred to the appearance of a shoot that would give the tree life, he was referring to Jesus.

To have the spirit of fear of the Lord does not mean to be afraid of God. Rather, it signifies having a heart that is full of respect for the greatness of the Creator.

Hope is an attitude by which Christians live with the confidence that God will always support us. God made this promise in many ways, but especially when he sent us his son, Jesus Christ.

The patriarchs were the ancestors of the people of Israel. Abraham, Isaac and Jacob were all known by this name. They received the promise that the people would become a great nation.

John the Baptist was the son of Zechariah and Elizabeth, who was a cousin of the Virgin Mary. He preached that the Messiah was about to arrive. He was called John the Baptist because those who were converted by his preaching were baptized in order to prepare themselves for the coming of the Saviour.

The Pharisees and the Sadducees were people who belonged to two Jewish religious sects. Pharisees were very strict and believed religion consisted in obeying the rules, sometimes forgetting that love is the greatest rule. The Sadducees did not believe in the resurrection of the dead.

Untying and carrying the sandals of a visitor was a lowly job for a slave or servant. John the Baptist shows how great Jesus is by saying he, John, is not worthy to carry Jesus' sandals — not worthy even to be Jesus' servant.

December 15

3rd Sunday of Advent

The wilderness and the dry land shall be glad,
the desert shall rejoice and blossom;
like the crocus it shall blossom abundantly,
and rejoice with joy and singing.
The glory of Lebanon shall be given to it,
the majesty of Carmel and Sharon.
They shall see the glory of the Lord,
the majesty of our God.

Strengthen the weak hands,
and make firm the feeble knees.
Say to those who are of a fearful heart,
"Be strong, do not fear!
Here is your God.
He will come with vengeance,
with terrible recompense.
He will come and save you."

Then the eyes of the blind shall be opened,
and the ears of the deaf unstopped;
then the lame shall leap like a deer,
and the tongue of the mute sing for joy.

And the ransomed of the Lord shall return,
and come to Zion with singing;
everlasting joy shall be upon their heads;
they shall obtain joy and gladness,
and sorrow and sighing shall flee away.

The word of the Lord. **Thanks be to God.**

R̰ **Lord, come and save us.**

or **Alleluia!**

It is the Lord who keeps faith forever,
who executes justice for the oppressed;
who gives food to the hungry.
The Lord sets the prisoners free. R̰

The Lord opens the eyes of the blind
and lifts up those who are bowed down;
the Lord loves the righteous
and watches over the strangers. R̰

The Lord upholds the orphan and the widow,
but the way of the wicked he brings to ruin.
The Lord will reign forever,
your God, O Zion, for all generations. R̰

A reading from the Letter of Saint James (5.7-10)

Be patient, brothers and sisters, until the coming of the Lord. The farmer waits for the precious crop from the earth, being patient with it until it receives the early and the late rains. You also must be patient. Strengthen your hearts, for the coming of the Lord is near.

Brothers and sisters, do not grumble against one another, so that you may not be judged. See, the Judge is standing at the doors! As an example of suffering and patience, brothers and sisters, take the Prophets who spoke in the name of the Lord.

The word of the Lord. **Thanks be to God.**

When John the Baptist heard in prison about the deeds of the Christ, he sent word by his disciples who said to Jesus, "Are you the one who is to come, or are we to wait for another?"

Jesus answered them, "Go and tell John what you hear and see: the blind receive their sight, the lame walk, the lepers are cleansed, the deaf hear, the dead are raised, and the poor have good news brought to them. And blessed is anyone who takes no offence at me."

As they went away, Jesus began to speak to the crowds about John: "What did you go out into the wilderness to look at? A reed shaken by the wind? What then did you go out to see? Someone dressed in soft robes? Look, those who wear soft robes are in royal palaces. What then did you go out to see? A Prophet? Yes, I tell you, and more than a Prophet. This is the one about whom it is written, 'See, I am sending my messenger ahead of you, who will prepare your way before you.'

"Truly I tell you, among those born of women no one has arisen greater than John the Baptist; yet the least in the kingdom of heaven is greater than he."

The Gospel of the Lord.
Praise to you, Lord Jesus Christ.

A crocus is among the first flowers that bloom in springtime.

Lebanon is a country at the eastern end of the Mediterranean Sea, bordering on modern-day Israel.

Carmel refers to a coastal mountain in Israel (see map, page 328). Mount Carmel marks the northern reach of the plain of Sharon, a flat region that includes the modern city of Tel Aviv.

The majesty of a king is his grandeur and power.

In the Old Testament there are many stories of battles and wars. Vengeance, which is a terrible thing, means getting even with someone by hitting them back after they have offended or hurt you. In this instance, the writer is trying to encourage the people to believe in God, who will eventually come to their aid.

If someone is oppressed then they are being very badly treated by others. Oppression deadens the soul and must be opposed by working for peace and justice.

The coming of the Lord is a reference to the Second Coming of Jesus. The first Christians thought that Jesus would be returning in their own lifetime, and so they understood this phrase in a very literal sense.

A reed is a thin shoot of a plant, often found near water.

Prophets were holy men and women who spoke publicly against poverty and injustice, and criticized the people whenever they refused to listen to God's word. Many of the books of the Old Testament were written by prophets (Isaiah, Jeremiah, Amos, and Micah, for example).

4th Sunday of Advent

A reading from the book of the Prophet Isaiah (7.10-14)

The Lord spoke to Ahaz, saying, "Ask a sign of the Lord your God; let it be deep as Sheol or high as heaven." But Ahaz said, "I will not ask, and I will not put the Lord to the test."

Then Isaiah said: "Hear then, O house of David! Is it too little for you to weary the people, that you weary my God also? Therefore the Lord himself will give you a sign. Look, the young woman is with child and shall bear a son, and shall name him Emmanuel."

The word of the Lord. **Thanks be to God.**

Psalm 24

R̰. **May the Lord come in; he is king of glory.**

The earth is the Lord's and all that is in it,
the world, and those who live in it;
for he has founded it on the seas,
and established it on the rivers. R̰.

Who shall ascend the hill of the Lord?
And who shall stand in his holy place?
Someone who has clean hands and a pure heart,
who does not lift up their soul to what is false. R̰.

That person will receive blessing from the Lord,
and vindication from the God of their salvation.
Such is the company of those who seek him,
who seek the face of the God of Jacob. R̰.

A reading from the Letter of Saint Paul to the Romans (1.1-7)

From Paul, a servant of Jesus Christ, called to be an Apostle, set apart for the Gospel of God, which God promised beforehand through his Prophets in the holy Scriptures: the Gospel concerning his Son, who was descended from David according to the flesh and was declared to be Son of God with power

308

according to the spirit of holiness by resurrection from the dead, Jesus Christ our Lord.

Through Christ we have received grace and apostleship to bring about the obedience of faith among all the Gentiles for the sake of his name, including yourselves who are called to belong to Jesus Christ.

To all God's beloved in Rome, who are called to be saints: Grace to you and peace from God our Father and the Lord Jesus Christ.

The word of the Lord. **Thanks be to God.**

A reading from the holy Gospel according to Matthew (1.18-24)

The birth of Jesus the Christ took place in this way. When his mother Mary had been engaged to Joseph, but before they lived together, she was found to be with child from the Holy Spirit. Her husband Joseph, being a righteous man and unwilling to expose her to public disgrace, planned to dismiss her quietly.

But just when he had resolved to do this, an Angel of the Lord appeared to him in a dream and said, "Joseph, son of David, do not be afraid to take Mary as your wife, for the child conceived in her is from the Holy Spirit. She will bear a son, and you are to name him Jesus, for he will save his people from their sins."

All this took place to fulfill what had been spoken by the Lord through the Prophet: "Look, the virgin shall conceive and bear a son, and they shall name him Emmanuel," which means, "God is with us." When Joseph awoke from sleep, he did as the Angel of the Lord commanded him; he took her as his wife.

The Gospel of the Lord. **Praise to you, Lord Jesus Christ.**

Ahaz was a king of Israel who was not well thought of. He was not true to the covenant with the Lord, he worshipped other gods that he himself had created and he closed the temple.

When the prophet Isaiah spoke to the house of David, he was speaking to all the Israelites. This was one of the names by which all the people of Israel were known.

The Letter of Saint Paul to the Romans is the longest surviving letter that Saint Paul wrote. The Christians who lived in Rome belonged to a small community. Paul wanted to travel to preach in Spain and stop on the way in Rome to visit the Christians. He sent this letter ahead in order to encourage them, and to remind them of the teachings of Jesus.

The word Gospel means the whole message that Jesus brought us. It is a word meaning the "Good News."

Apostleship is a mission that God gave to Saint Paul, to announce the Good News of the resurrection of Jesus — that Jesus conquered death. This is also the mission of all Christians.

The Gentiles are people who are not Jewish.

Saint Matthew was the author of one of the four gospels. This story clearly tells us about the life of Jesus and emphasizes that he is the promised Messiah, and that the Church is now the Chosen People, the new Israel.

Joseph and Mary were engaged, but they did not live together before marriage. For this reason Joseph was surprised that Mary was expecting a baby.

The Nativity of the Lord
Christmas

The people who walked in darkness have seen a great light;
those who lived in a land of deep darkness —
on them light has shone.
You have multiplied the nation,
you have increased its joy;
they rejoice before you
as with joy at the harvest,
as people exult when dividing plunder.

For the yoke of their burden,
and the bar across their shoulders,
the rod of their oppressor,
you have broken as on the day of Midian.

For a child has been born for us,
a son given to us;
authority rests upon his shoulders;
and he is named
Wonderful Counsellor, Mighty God,
Everlasting Father, Prince of Peace.

His authority shall grow continually,
and there shall be endless peace
for the throne of David and his kingdom.
He will establish and uphold it
with justice and with righteousness
from this time onward and forevermore.
The zeal of the Lord of hosts will do this.

The word of the Lord. **Thanks be to God.**

R. **Today is born our Saviour, Christ the Lord.**

O sing to the Lord a new song;
sing to the Lord, all the earth.
Sing to the Lord, bless his name;
tell of his salvation from day to day. R.

Declare his glory among the nations,
his marvellous works among all the peoples.
For great is the Lord, and greatly to be praised;
he is to be revered above all gods. R.

Let the heavens be glad, and let the earth rejoice;
let the sea roar, and all that fills it;
let the field exult, and everything in it.
Then shall all the trees of the forest sing for joy. R.

Rejoice before the Lord; for he is coming,
for he is coming to judge the earth.
He will judge the world with righteousness,
and the peoples with his truth. R.

A reading from the Letter of Saint Paul to Titus
(2.11-14)

Beloved: The grace of God has appeared, bringing salvation to all, training us to renounce impiety and worldly passions, and in the present age to live lives that are self-controlled, upright, and godly, while we wait for the blessed hope and the manifestation of the glory of our great God and Saviour, Jesus Christ.

He it is who gave himself for us that he might redeem us from all iniquity and purify for himself a people of his own who are zealous for good deeds.

The word of the Lord. **Thanks be to God.**

In those days a decree went out from Caesar Augustus that all the world should be registered. This was the first registration and was taken while Quirinius was governor of Syria. All went to their own towns to be registered. Joseph also went from the town of Nazareth in Galilee to Judea, to the city of David called Bethlehem, because he was descended from the house and family of David. He went to be registered with Mary, to whom he was engaged and who was expecting a child.

While they were there, the time came for her to deliver her child. And she gave birth to her firstborn son and wrapped him in swaddling clothes, and laid him in a manger, because there was no place for them in the inn.

In that region there were shepherds living in the fields, keeping watch over their flock by night. Then an Angel of the Lord stood before them, and the glory of the Lord shone around them, and they were terrified. But the Angel said to them, "Do not be afraid; for see — I am bringing you good news of great joy for all the people: to you is born this day in the city of David a Saviour, who is the Christ, the Lord. This will be a sign for you: you will find a child wrapped in swaddling clothes and lying in a manger."

And suddenly there was with the Angel a multitude of the heavenly host, praising God and saying, "Glory to God in the highest heaven, and on earth peace among those whom he favours!"

When the Angels had left them and gone into heaven, the shepherds said to one another, "Let us go now to Bethlehem and see this thing that has taken place, which the Lord has made known to us." So they went with haste and found Mary and Joseph, and the child lying in the manger.

The Gospel of the Lord.
**Praise to you,
Lord Jesus Christ.**

KEY WORDS

Christmas Day is celebrated on December 25th, but the Christmas season lasts for three weeks, ending with the Baptism of Jesus in January. The liturgical colour for this season is white, the colour of joy and celebration.

Prophets like Isaiah were good men and women who spoke for God. Sometimes their messages were demanding: they asked people to change their lives and attitudes to grow closer to God. At other times, they brought words of comfort.

We sing for joy because our hearts are full of happiness: God has come to be with his people. In today's psalm, we see that all creation — even the trees! — rejoice and glory in the Lord.

A manger is a wooden crate filled with hay to feed the animals in a stable. The baby Jesus was placed in a manger soon after he was born. It is amazing that God would choose to be born in such a simple place.

An Angel of the Lord is a messenger of God. Angels appear many times in the Bible, as we see angels revealing God's plan in the lives of Jesus, Mary and Joseph.

Glory to God in the highest and on earth peace to all people!

Merry Christmas!

Holy Family of Jesus, Mary and Joseph

A reading from the book of Sirach (3.2-6, 12-14)

The Lord honours a father above his children,
and he confirms a mother's rights over her sons.
Whoever honours their father atones for sins
and gains preservation from them;
when they pray, they will be heard.
Whoever respects their mother
is like one who lays up treasure.
The person who honours their father
will have joy in their own children,
and when they pray they will be heard.
Whoever respects their father will have a long life,
and whoever honours their mother obeys the Lord.

My child, help your father in his old age,
and do not grieve him as long as he lives.
Even if his mind fails, be patient with him;
because you have all your faculties,
do not despise him all the days of his life.
For kindness to your father will not be forgotten,
and will be credited to you against your sins —
a house raised in justice for you.

The word of the Lord. **Thanks be to God.**

Psalm 128

R̥ **Blessed is everyone who fears the Lord.**

or **Blessed is everyone who fears the Lord, who walks in his ways.**

Blessed is everyone who fears the Lord,
who walks in his ways.
You shall eat the fruit of the labour of your hands;
you shall be happy, and it shall go well with you. R̥

Your wife will be like a fruitful vine
within your house;
your children will be like olive shoots
around your table. R̥

Thus shall the man be blessed who fears the Lord.
The Lord bless you from Zion.
May you see the prosperity of Jerusalem
all the days of your life. R̥

The shorter reading ends at the asterisks.

Brothers and sisters: As God's chosen ones, holy and beloved, clothe yourselves with compassion, kindness, humility, meekness, and patience. Bear with one another and, if anyone has a complaint against another, forgive each other; just as the Lord has forgiven you, so you also must forgive. Above all, clothe yourselves with love, which binds everything together in perfect harmony. And let the peace of Christ rule in your hearts, to which indeed you were called in the one body. And be thankful.

Let the word of Christ dwell in you richly; teach and admonish one another in all wisdom; and with gratitude in your hearts sing Psalms, hymns, and spiritual songs to God. And whatever you do, in word or deed, do everything in the name of the Lord Jesus, giving thanks to God the Father through him.

***

Wives, be subject to your husbands, as is fitting in the Lord. Husbands, love your wives and never treat them harshly. Children, obey your parents in everything, for this is your acceptable duty in the Lord. Fathers, do not provoke your children, or they may lose heart.

The word of the Lord. **Thanks be to God.**

After the wise men had left, an Angel of the Lord appeared to Joseph in a dream and said, "Get up, take the child and his mother, and flee to Egypt, and remain there until I tell you; for Herod is about to search for the child, to destroy him." Then Joseph got up, took the child and his mother by night, and went to Egypt, and remained there until the death of Herod. This was to fulfill what had been spoken by the Lord through the Prophet, "Out of Egypt I have called my son."

When Herod died, an Angel of the Lord suddenly appeared in a dream to Joseph in Egypt and said, "Get up, take the child and his mother, and go to the land of Israel, for those who were seeking the child's life are dead." Then Joseph got up, took the child and his mother, and went to the land of Israel.

But when he heard that Archelaus was ruling over Judea in place of his father Herod, he was afraid to go there. And after being warned in a dream, he went away to the district of Galilee. There he made his home in a town called Nazareth, so that what had been spoken through the Prophets might be fulfilled, "He will be called a Nazorean."

The Gospel of the Lord. **Praise to you, Lord Jesus Christ.**

In the Bible the phrase "obey the Lord" is not used to make us fear God. How could we fear such a wonderful parent? Obey the Lord means to recognize how great God is, how good, how very important and that we should show tenderness and respect to God.

A vine is a plant that bears grapes. A fruitful vine gives many grapes. In biblical times, a woman was considered blessed by God when she had children.

Someone who is holy is set apart for God's service. All of us Christians are chosen by God since the time of our baptism, when we were united with Jesus.

Giving thanks to God is a task for all Christians. Gratitude is a virtue, best expressed when we show compassion for others and try to be of assistance to those who are suffering. In Greek, the word for giving thanks is "eucharist."

The wise men were scholars who came from the East. They were most likely people dedicated to studying the stars. They told Herod they were following an unusually bright star and they thought it must herald the birth of a king.

This is a reference to Herod the Great, a friend of the Romans. He governed many lands. He was known for his cruelty as well as for his lack of interest in religion. His son Herod Antipas was the man who was in Jerusalem on the day that Jesus was crucified.

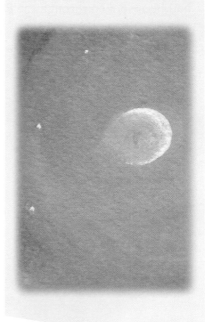

Morning & Evening Prayers

Morning Prayer

Dear God, we thank you for this day.
We thank you for our families and friends.
We thank you for our classmates.
Be with us as we work and play today.
Help us always to be kind to each other.
We pray in the name of the Father,
and of the Son and of the Holy Spirit. Amen.

(Heather Reid, *Let's Pray! Prayers for the Elementary Classroom.*
Ottawa; Novalis: 2006)

Child's Bedtime Prayer

Now I lay me down to sleep,
I pray you, Lord, your child to keep.
Your love will guard me through the night
and wake me with the morning light. Amen.

God Hear My Prayer

God in heaven hear my prayer,
keep me in your loving care.
Be my guide in all I do,
bless all those who love me too. Amen.

More Prayers

Prayer for Friends

Loving God, you are the best friend we can have.

We ask today that you help us to be good friends
to each other.

Help us to be fair, kind and unselfish.

Keep our friends safe and happy.

Bless us and bless all friends in this community.

We pray in the name of Jesus,

who was always the friend of children. Amen.

(Heather Reid, *Let's Pray! Prayers for the Elementary Classroom.*
Ottawa; Novalis: 2006)

In the Silence

If we really want to pray,
we must first learn to listen,
for in the silence of the heart,
God speaks.

(Blessed Teresa of Calcutta, 1910-1997)

Family Prayer

Father, what love you have given us.
May we love as you would have us love.
Teach us to be kind to each other,
patient and gentle with one another.
Help us to bear all things together,
to see in our love, your love,
through Christ our Lord. Amen.

Prayer for the Birthday Child

May God bless you with every good gift
and surround you with love and happiness.
May Jesus be your friend and guide
all the days of your life.
May the Spirit of God guide your footsteps
in the path of truth. Amen.

Prayer for Pets

Dear Father, hear and bless
your beasts and singing birds,
and guard with care and tenderness
small things that have no words. Amen.

When Someone Has Died

Lord God, hear our cries.
Grant us comfort in our sadness,
gently wipe away our tears,
and give us courage in the days ahead.
We ask this through Christ our Lord. Amen.

Traditional Prayers

Lord's Prayer

Our Father, who art in heaven,
hallowed be thy name;
thy kingdom come,
thy will be done on earth as it is in heaven.
Give us this day our daily bread,
and forgive us our trespasses,
as we forgive those who trespass against us;
and lead us not into temptation,
but deliver us from evil. Amen.

Hail Mary

Hail Mary, full of grace,
the Lord is with you.
Blessed are you among women and
blessed is the fruit of your womb, Jesus.
Holy Mary, Mother of God,
pray for us sinners,
now and at the hour of our death. Amen.

Glory Be to the Father

Glory be to the Father,
and to the Son,
and to the Holy Spirit.
As it was in the beginning,
is now, and ever shall be,
world without end. Amen.

Mealtime Prayers

Grace before Meals

Bless us, O Lord,
and these your gifts
which we are about to receive
from your bounty.
Through Christ our Lord. Amen.

* * *

For food in a world where many walk in hunger,
for friends in a world where many walk alone,
for faith in a world where many walk in fear,
we give you thanks, O God. Amen.

* * *

God is great, God is good!
Let us thank God for our food. Amen.

* * *

Be present at our table, Lord.
Be here and everywhere adored.
Your creatures bless
and grant that we may feast
in paradise with you. Amen.

Grace after Meals

We give you thanks, Almighty God,
for these and all the benefits
we receive from your bounty.
Through Christ our Lord. Amen.

* * *

Palestine 2,000 years ago

When Jesus lived here...

- Palestine was a small country, occupied by soldiers of the Roman Empire. Jerusalem was the capital city.
- The country already had a very long history. It was in a part of the world we call the "cradle of civilization."
- Travellers from all around the Mediterranean Sea and the Far East passed through Palestine. Neighbours and visitors included Egyptians, Phoenicians, Syrians, Parthians, Nabateans, Greeks and many others.
- Many citizens understood several languages, including Aramaic, Hebrew, Greek and Latin.

Three horizontal divisions:

- North: Galilee (area #2 on the map) is an area of pleasant weather. Jesus spent most of his life here.
- Central: Samaria (area #3) reaches from the sea coast to the mountain range.
- South: Judea (area #1) is a mountainous region with harsh, dry weather.

Four geographic regions (vertical strips):

- The coastal plain: a broad, flat section along the coast, wide in the south and narrower in the north. Summers here are hot and humid.
- The mountain chain: dry and desert in the south; more fertile valleys in the north.
- The deep ravine: the Jordan Rift Valley splits the mountain range in two, with the Sea of Galilee at one end of the rift and the Jordan River flowing south to the Dead Sea at the other end.
- The plateau: a high, flat area beyond the mountains on the east side of the Jordan River.

Palestine today:

Most of the country where Jesus lived is now called 'Israel.' It is bordered by Lebanon to the north, Syria and Jordan to the east, and Egypt to the south.

1. Judea	5. Perea	
2. Galilee	6. Decapolis	EGYPT
3. Samaria	7. Syria and Tetrarchy of Philip	
4. Phoenicia	8. Idumea	